Cultural Foundations of Iranian Politics

M. Reza Behnam

University of Utah Press
Salt Lake City

Library of Congress Cataloging-in-Publication Data

Behnam, M. Reza, 1945–
   Cultural foundations of Iranian politics.

   Bibliography: p.
   Includes index.
   1. Iran—Politics and government.   2. Politics and
culture—Iran.   3. Social structure—Iran.   4. Islam
and state—Iran.   5. Iran—History—Revolution, 1979.
I. Title.
JQ1785.B44   1986   306'.2'0955   86-15871
ISBN 0-87480-265-2

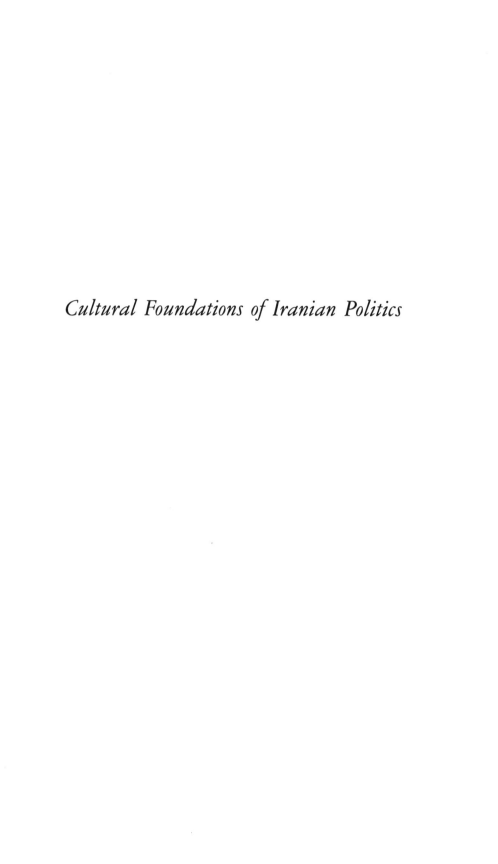

Cultural Foundations of Iranian Politics

To
Anna and August
whose visionary world
gave me the freedom to think

Contents

Preface

One of the most important questions a political scientist can ask is why the government of a country behaves the way it does. A thoughtful response requires research and care and perhaps theoretical premises which may be open to criticism by those who prefer to undertake research based on isolated events, periods, and personalities. In this study, I have analyzed Iran's political system holistically. Iran often appears to be an enigmatic country, especially to the West; this study may dispel some of the misunderstandings.

My intent in writing the book is to establish a relationship between the dominant cultural patterns of Iranian society and the form and function of the political system. It analyzes the political system of Iran through the use of cultural variables. It proposes that we can more clearly understand the political system by looking at significant, widely held, and enduring societal norms and values. It examines how certain cultural norms and orientations influence Iran's politics.

The study focuses on the historical, religious, and social dimensions of Iranian political culture from monarchy to the Islamic government. Although the form of government in Iran has changed over the years, especially beginning in 1979, political culture patterns have not. An awareness of their dominating role contributes substantially to our understanding of Iran's ever-evolving political system.

In transliteration, a modified version of the Library of Congress system was followed. Spellings of Arabic and Persian words widely known in the English-speaking world are in their familiar form and are not italicized; those that are not commonly used are italicized only on first use.

I am grateful to a number of people who assisted in bringing the manuscript to its final form. I am indebted to Dr. W. Parkes Riley for his intellectual support and critiques of early versions of the manuscript. Also, thanks and affection go to Walter W. Slocum, Ruth South, and Robert R. Lockhard, librarians at the University of Oregon, whose expertise was invaluable in my research efforts. Sincere thanks are due Professor James A. Bill, who read an early version of the manuscript and offered helpful comments. My appreciation also goes to the staff of the University of Utah Press. Of course, none of the individuals thanked above are responsible for any deficiencies or interpretations found in the book.

Cultural Foundations of Iranian Politics

I

Introduction

There is much about Iran that is enigmatic. It underwent an unusual revolution, deposing a monarch and political apparatus thought almost unassailable. It had the unprecedented pluck to defy and vilify a superpower—the United States—after the Islamic Revolution; and it has altered the strategic balance in the Middle East, stirring strong feelings around the world. The political history of Iran has always been interesting, but contemporary events have made it even more important. This book focuses on the culture of Iran to gain insight into its politics, past and present, inquiring into the nature, role, and relationships of dominant, long-lasting cultural variables as they affect the structure, operation, and development of the political system.

Politics is a distillation of certain fundamental qualities of the more general culture. Thus, the shared beliefs and collective values of a people and the form of government are unified by the concept of culture. As one writer comments, "by focusing on basic value orientations —often implicit assumptions about the nature of man and the nature of physical reality—we may find a set of political attitudes that, though not structured as the political philosopher might structure them, nevertheless have a definite and significant structure."[1]

This chapter reviews the concepts of culture and political culture.

THE CONCEPT OF CULTURE

A basic premise of anthropological investigation is that individuals learn the values and norms of their society. *Culture* is the term used to explicate the unique values of a people that are widely shared and transmitted from one generation to the next. Culture is expressed through behavior and entails both the internal, the ideas, and the external, the social action they motivate.

Culture itself is a configurational concept, a term used to help understand the regularities in human events. Each cultural system tends to have a logic of its own that weaves the various elements into a related and interdependent whole. There is a certain pattern to cultural values and behavior. Action patterns as well as motivational systems of individuals within a society are influenced by culture.[2]

Culture consists of accumulated ideas that provide the rules, techniques, and understandings necessary for continuing survival of the group. It is the complex whole that includes knowledge, beliefs, art, myths, morals, law, customs, and any other capabilities and habits acquired by a member of society.

As a system, culture functions to give coherence, meaning, and predictability to a society. With shared ideas, behavior becomes somewhat predictable, a prerequisite for organized social living. The valued ends and sanctioned means of behavior appropriate for members of a distinct social system are communicated to each new generation; generally, individuals adjust to the traditionally defined expectations of their group. Although factors such as biological makeup and family influence create uniquely different individuals, members of a society are involved in a particular societal paradigm that expresses itself in belief systems, cultural norms and values, and behavior patterns, passed on by imitation and/or instruction from one generation to the next.

Excluding material items, culture is a patterned system of shared values and understandings that mold and influence the behavior of members of a society. Although culture shapes social action, it does not fully determine it. Culture merely prescribes the ways drives and needs might be gratified.[3] Members of a society are at once conveyors of culture and cultural innovators. The strict deterministic view of culture (like that of Leslie White, for example) overemphasizes culture as an overwhelming force that determines all social response.[4] If culture were an inexorable determining force and other factors—technology, environment, and individual personality—inconsequential, change would be ruled out.

All cultures change, but some change more slowly and to a lesser extent than others. Change must be systematic and ordered so as not to destroy the existing fabric of society. All cultures have basic needs for shelter, established order, predictability, shared cosmology, and fulfillment of aesthetic impulses. It is the basic needs working together as a system that shape a culture. These basic needs are mediated by innovations, and their fulfillment decides culture change. Cultural change might be effected from within and without: internally, through individual personalities; externally, through contact with more potent culture(s). Although societies change over time, traditional understandings are less likely to change.

Culture is a concept developed to explicate the differences in lifestyles and values among various social systems. There are a great many definitions of culture.[5] Inherent in most of them is the stress on a set of patterned values that, when added together, define a total way of life for a people.

It was Saint-Simon who recognized that institutions are the products of ideas. The institutions of a society reflect the cultural ideas and norms inherent in it. Culture influences sociopolitical action, the political process, and institutions.

THE CONCEPT OF POLITICAL CULTURE

Much has been written of political culture since Gabriel Almond first effectively used the term in 1956, asserting that "every political system is embedded in a particular pattern of orientations to political action. I have found it useful to refer to this as the political culture."[6] The term *political culture* finds its origins in the sociological and anthropological work of individuals such as Ruth Benedict, Margaret Mead, Clyde Kluckhohn, Abram Kardiner, Ralph Linton, and others who developed the concepts of culture and personality. It was their general contention that members of a given culture share certain common and distinct ways of viewing reality and regulating social conduct that differ from those of other cultural groups. The question of why the political system of a nation operates the way it does and consideration of the belief system of members of a nation as an important factor are not new to political literature. Contributions to the study of political culture can be traced to the works of Machiavelli, Montesquieu, Rousseau, Tocqueville, Bagehot, and Max Weber, and as far back as the Greeks.

The concept of culture was pervasive in the social sciences for years. But it was wartime concern with understanding the behavior of foreign nations, particularly the enemy, that stimulated the infusion of new ideas into the field of political science.[7] Also, the emergence of a host of new sovereign states raised questions about the conduct of politics and the nature of these differences. Essentially, the discipline was slow to incorporate the concept of culture.

As noted earlier, Gabriel Almond first introduced the concept of political culture in 1956, taking the position that beliefs, feelings, and values significantly influence political behavior and that these elements are the product of socialization. Two years later, Samuel H. Beer and Adam B. Ulam, in their edited comparative politics text, centered upon the concept of political culture.[8] The most renowned empirical study of political culture is Almond and Verba's *The Civic Culture* (1963), in which political attitudes in five countries (the United States, Great Britain, West Germany, Italy, and Mexico) are analyzed. In their investigation, the authors distinguish parochial, subject, and participant cultures, basing this classification upon the degree of member participation in the political sector of society. Almond and Verba suggest that the above-named countries have a "common political culture" but are separate and different kinds of political systems. Based on their analysis, the authors constructed a model of an ideal democratic culture—"the civic culture"—of consensus, diversity, and pluralism.[9] They describe an allegiant participant civic culture in which political culture and political structure are congruent, and in which the maintenance of more traditional attitudes (subject, parochial, and nonparticipant political orientations) and their fusion with the participant orientation "lead to a balanced political culture in which political activity, involvement, and rationality exist but are balanced by passivity, traditionality, and commitment to parochial values."[10] Almond and Verba's study emphasizes patterns or orientations to political actions constituting a political culture. Although *The Civic Culture* reflects a certain ethnocentrism, it does mark a major advance in developing the concept of political culture as a useful tool in comparative politics.

Lucian Pye and Sidney Verba elaborated on the concept in their collaborative investigation of varieties of political culture, entitled *Political Culture and Political Development.*[11] Concentrating on political development themes, Pye discusses the various ways the concept of political culture can help explain developmental processes and problems. Verba attempts to delineate the salient dimensions of political culture to include the sense of national identity, attitudes toward oneself as participant, attitudes toward fellow citizens, attitudes and expectations regarding governmental output and performance, and knowledge of and attitudes toward the political process of decision making. Pye sees the concept of political culture as a valuable approach that combines individual psychology and collective sociology, well adapted for comparing and classifying political systems in terms relevant for understanding the character of political development and change.[12]

Almond and Verba, in *The Civic Culture Revisited* (1980), present a series of essays that assess the impact of their original work.[13] As Verba points out, *"The Civic Culture* used survey techniques to study citizen attitudes and values within a set of quite varied nations to deal with the macropolitical problem of democratic stability."[14] Their original work (1963) was a bold undertaking that set the stage for employment of the concept of political culture where concepts such as public opinion, political ideology, national ethos, and the like were once used.

As used by most political scientists, the concept of political culture comes from Gabriel Almond's observation cited earlier in this section. Lucian Pye describes political culture as consisting of "only those critical but widely shared beliefs and sentiments that form the 'particular patterns of orientation' that give order and form to the political process. In sum, the political culture provides structure and meaning to the political sphere in the same manner as culture in general gives coherence and integration to social life."[15] Political culture for Sidney Verba is "the system of empirical beliefs, expressive symbols, and values which defines the situation in which political action takes place. It provides the subjective orientation to politics."[16] However defined, the concept of political culture has provided a means of incorporating anthropological, sociological, and psychological theory into the study of political systems.

The emphasis in contemporary political analysis on the concept of political culture signals an effort to return to the study of the total political system without discarding the benefits to be derived from the psychological or subjective dimensions of politics. The behavioral revolution has reached into political science, infusing it with new political theories.

THEORETICAL CONSIDERATIONS REGARDING POLITICAL CULTURE

Certain generalizations about the structure of political cultures are recognized. Among these is the existence of a plurality of political cultures in a given society. In no society does there seem to be a single uniform political culture; in all polities there is distinction between the power holders, or elite, and the masses. For example, in India we see a relatively homogeneous elite culture and a fragmented mass culture distinguished by caste, religion, and language. Another division in political culture separates those more acculturated to modern ways from those who are more aligned to traditional patterns of life. This is especially relevant in transitional societies in which the belief systems stress modernity in politics and economics, but these beliefs are markedly different from the more traditional orientations associated with other aspects of life, causing strain within society.

Another generalization about the concept of political culture is that it implies "an underlying and latent coherence in political life."[17] Governments come and go, but political cultures endure. A pertinent example of the durability of political culture can be extracted from the experience of the USSR, which is a dramatic case of planned cultural change. The Russian political experience until the Revolution of 1917 centered around the tsarist regime. With the Revolution came an eventual change in orientation to governmental processes. But deeply rooted political culture variables, particularly authority patterns (ruler-subject pattern), did not change and affected the nascent political system. So today we see in the Soviet Union a somewhat transformed and attenuated form of communism, certainly not that envisioned by Marx and Lenin. Although the abrogation of class differences was the revolutionary ideal, what emerged was a powerful ruling class, at times with leaders not totally unlike those of tsarist Russia. The traditional understandings of the Russian people about power and authority seem to have had a significant effect upon the political system that developed in postrevolutionary Russia.

Tentative observations on Communist attempts to create new political values and to cast aside old values suggest that "the attempt to create a new socialist man . . . has been on the whole a depressing failure. . . ."[18] In this vein it is also noted that:

> There is a substantial and significant contrast between those countries in which Russian influence puts sharp limits on the possibility of change, and those countries (China, Cuba and Yugoslavia) which are independent. The degree of divergence in these countries is very great. Cuba may be a case merely of incomplete convergence, but in the other two countries free of Russian dominance the Communist system has been wholly remodelled in ways powerfully influenced by national tradition.[19]

If a system is to endure, it must do certain things. The function of a culture system is to provide the rules, techniques, and understandings necessary for the continued survival of the group. Culture also forges a link between the values and behavior patterns of members of a political system and the form and action of government in that system. Political culture involves the fundamental collective understandings a society has about power, authority, and action. It is a society's significant beliefs and orientations that define the behavior of its members and affect the operation, maintenance, or dissolution of a political system. In keeping with this idea of political culture, Pye observes that "deep cultural sentiments outlast the transitory shifts in power structures, and they condition the entire approach of a people in their dealings with and manipulations of power."[20] The concept of political culture is a valuable instrument for understanding political behavior and structural changes.

DEFINING POLITICAL CULTURE IN RELATION TO IRANIAN SOCIETY

Although the political culture of Iran has certain features in common with that of other countries, it also has certain values, orientations, and norms that make it unique. The intent of this study is to show just how the particular characteristics of Iranian culture have shaped the political experience of Iran in recent times.

There seem to be two broad types of political culture that predominate in Iran, encompassing a multitude of diverse strands of behavior and action within the political structure: authoritarian and antiauthoritarian.[21] These two types of political culture have coexisted over time and have often been in overt conflict with each other. Authoritarian political culture in Iran involves submission and obedience to authority and acceptance of as well as belief in strong leadership. In *The Civic Culture*, Almond and Verba describe authoritarian political culture as subject political culture, which has a high frequency of orientations toward a differentiated political system beyond the individual's local environment and toward the outputs of that system. But orientations toward political participation and inputs into the political system remain very low. This description fits the authoritarian or subject political culture that has existed in Iran.

It is theorized that the authoritarian nature of Iranian political culture is derived from two sources: the hierarchical system of monarchical rule that prevailed for centuries and the hierarchical and dominant role of religion in social and political life. As we shall see, the antiauthoritarian political culture of Iran seems to find its roots in religion as well. First let us look briefly at the idea of authoritarian political culture in terms of the monarchical system of Iran. Monarchical rule was the norm of government in Iran until the spread of a revolutionary political culture in the twentieth century. Iran has traditionally resisted being dominated or influenced by foreign powers. Protecting and expanding borders was the preoccupation of monarchs of the past. Although ruled by the Arabs in the seventh and eighth centuries, Iranians maintained their national identity by assimilating an unorthodox brand of Islam, leading to the spread of Shi'ite Islam in the Iranian state. With the discovery of oil in 1908, Iran again found itself in the middle between two great powers (Great Britain and Russia), each contending for economic and political supremacy in the area. Later this competition for Iran's resources shifted from Great Britain to the United States. Due to this long history of encroachment and exploitation, Iran developed a deeply rooted xenophobia and distrust of foreign powers. Colonization was tenaciously resisted. Rulers who faithfully guarded Iranian sovereignty had the general support of the polity, which further entrenched monarchical authority and authoritarian political culture.

Acquiescence to monarchical authority in Iran was based on the existence of a type of legitimacy rooted in tradition or charisma, or a combination of the two. That the monarchical system existed for centuries provided a type of legitimacy and ensured its continued survival. The traditional idea of monarchy combined with the charisma of a respected leader was a powerful force in the preservation of authoritarian political culture. Iranian history is replete with praise for the exploits and courage of popular leaders who enhanced the position and esteem of Iranian civilization.

Almond and Verba's definition of a subject political culture is significant for the political culture of Iran in that there are pervasive expectations of the larger political authority, while participation and inputs into the political process have been essentially minimal. One of the primary expectations of the Iranian polity is that political authority will protect the nation from foreign influence and domination. This factor has had a profound effect on the nature of authority in Iran past and present.

Religion also seems to have contributed to the authoritarian/subject political culture of Iran. Elements within Ithna Ashari Shiʿism (Twelve Imam Shiʿism) such as absolutism, hereditary leadership, elitism, and obedience have enhanced the notion of authority. The role of the Imamate (with its corollary of obedience), discussed in chapter 3, appears to play a part in the authority patterns developed in the country.

The other dominant factor in Iranian political culture is described herein as antiauthoritarianism. During periods of Iranian history when certain moral or economic interests seemed threatened or violated, the polity sought change through group action. Historical evidence demonstrates an indigenous antiauthoritarian political culture in Iran, most clearly evident during the nineteenth and twentieth centuries: in the Constitutional Revolution of 1905–9 (and the events leading to it), in oil nationalization of the 1950s, and finally in the Islamic Revolution of 1978–79. Iranians have traditionally revealed a willingness to challenge authority, especially when economic interests or national integrity, or both, were at stake. This unwillingness to accept capricious rule has often been manifested in nonviolent ways, taking the form of mass demonstrations, boycotts, strikes, and the like. Iran's streets have traditionally been the scene of mass demonstrations against undesirable political authority, and its mosques have been sanctuaries where political dissent could be openly manifested, where otherwise suppressed. The Islamic Revolution exemplified the nonviolent, mass political expression of the Iranian people against what was perceived as illegitimate authority.

Iran has been a nation of independent groups, each wielding a certain degree of power. Before Reza Shah's rule, Iran had a decentralized class structure with tribal leaders, landlords, ulama, bazaar classes, bureaucrats, and a few intellectuals possessing considerable autonomy and power. Pahlavi rule brought centralization and a reduction in the independent power of these groups; but the growth in bureaucracy led to the rise of a new group, the professional middle class. The independent power of some of these groups was minimized, but their influence, although dormant at times, was always just under the surface and could be mobilized when needed. This is especially true in regard to the ulama and bazaar merchants, whose excellent and widespread communications with the masses created an influential power base capable of challenging authority.

One of the major challenges to political authority in Iran has been the power of religion. Hope for change and the establishment of just rule are underlying themes of Shi'ite Islam. As we shall see, the theology of Ithna Ashari Shi'ism asserts the imperfection of secular government, the Imamate being the model of perfection. The prerogative of the ulama in Iran is to guard the nation and the community of faithful against the corrupt power of the secular political authority. These ideas inherent in Shi'ite Islam have been a factor in shaping and motivating political action in Iran, and antiauthoritarianism has found expression in its ideals and religious leadership.

Within the authoritarian and antiauthoritarian political cultures of Iran is a vital element inherent in both—charismatic authority. Max Weber described charismatic authority as one of the ideal-typical reasons why leaders are obeyed by followers, from which political legitimacy derives. Charismatic authority is characterized by a belief in the superhuman qualities of a leader. Charismatic figures have quite frequently risen to political authority to direct the course of events during pivotal periods in the political history of Iran. Authority has a tenuous base in Iranian political culture; while accepting political authority, the polity has a general mistrust of it. This dichotomy appears to run deep.

It should be noted that these are not the only aspects of Iranian political culture; there are a multitude of diverse strands that give it a specific content and nature. Thus, in Iran there are strong antiauthoritarian yet equally strong proauthoritarian norms. No one political culture has become clearly dominant. Instead there seems to be an indigenous tension between the two. A divergent rather than definitive political culture characterizes the political experience of Iran. Parliamentarianism is a recent phenomenon in Iran, introduced in the twentieth century. The Iranian parliamentary system has more or less endured, but with difficulty, largely because of the rival authoritarian traditions, independent groups, and intrusion from outside forces.

The politics of contemporary Iran can better be understood by a recognition of the interplay among the varied types of political culture described to this point and more fully explored in the following pages. The discussion thus far has dealt with the justification and usefulness of the political culture approach. Since the theme of this study is the political culture of Iran, it now becomes necessary to look more closely at how to approach the study of political culture in Iran.

APPROACHES TO IRANIAN POLITICAL CULTURE

A cultural system is made up of a panoply of parts, and the same is true of political culture. In analyzing the political culture of Iran, one must decide upon the parts that seem most germane to understanding the system. In analyzing Iranian society, a number of enduring themes inherent in the cultural system that affect Iranian politics predominate. The following themes receive special attention in this study: (1) the legacy of authoritarianism, involving the monarchical system, religion, and the tradition of family; (2) the legacy of antiauthoritarianism, involving the special role of Shiʿite Islam and Iranian individualism. The following chapters focus on the historical, religious, and psychological dimensions of Iranian political culture. The time frame of the study is primarily from the late nineteenth century to the deposition of Mohammad Reza Pahlavi and the development of the Islamic Republic of Iran.

This study begins by analyzing the history of Iran, focusing on pivotal periods that enhance our understanding of Iranian political culture. In exploring the origin and nature of political culture, it is necessary to analyze the historical development of the system as a whole. We shall look at the political history of Iran not so much as a series of objective events, but as a series of events that reflect a cultural point of view. Also, chapter 2 discusses the role of the monarchical system in Iran over time, focusing upon the authoritarian nature of the Iranian political system. One aspect of the analysis is the legitimacy of the political system based on the polity's understanding of the role of the leader and expectations of government, plus the polity's view of its role in the political process. The memories passed from one generation to the next and the way they are assimilated and formed are critical to the political system. In this chapter an understanding of the political culture of Iran is developed by examining the past and observing how the political system has evolved over time.

Chapter 3 analyzes the role of religion and religious leaders in the sociopolitical life of the country. The subject of this chapter is the significance of religion as a symbol of national identity and wellspring of political action and change. Through the ages and in all societies, religion has provided a basis for the individual's sense of identity, and this is especially true in Iran, where religion has been the center of culture. This chapter explores the religious norms and values that contribute to Iran's political culture, as well as the economic and political role of Iran's religious leaders. The affinity between the sacred and secular is particularly important in Iran and has been the vehicle for sociopolitical change. There is an intimate association between religion and the political process; the depth of that relationship is considered in chapter 3.

Chapter 4 analyzes sociological linkages to the political system and deals with the psychological dimension of Iranian political culture; homogeneity, however, cannot be assumed. This section concentrates on the cultural variables, unique to the socialization process in Iran, that affect the operation of the political system. Specific attention is directed toward the Iranian family, education, and the literary-artistic milieu, based on the notion that the socialization process of a culture contributes to the spirit of politics. Among the factors that shape political culture are the "intensely private and personal experiences of individuals as they become members of first the society and then the polity."[22]

Some of the structural aspects of the Iranian political system, particularly during the reign of Mohammad Reza Pahlavi, are the subject of chapter 5. To understand the political culture of Iran, the regime's monopoly of power and techniques for preserving that power must be considered. During the 1970s, governmental outputs and the decision-making process came under question by the polity. This section discusses how the Pahlavi regime attempted to fulfill the basic needs of the society in the physical realm while manipulating the political-economic system, during the period of the 1950s to late 1970s. This epoch is important because the issues of legitimacy, political development, and change became crucial to the functioning of Iran's political system in the future.

The concluding chapter of this study focuses on the demise of an age-old political system and the creation of a new political order. The focus of analysis is not only the deposition of the Pahlavi regime and the monarchical system, but the creation of the Islamic Republic. In this final chapter we shall look at the foundations of the Islamic Revolution in terms of the political culture of Iran. It also offers a comparative analysis of the Constitutional Revolution and Islamic Revolution, examines the core of Iranian nationalism that gave impetus to the Islamic Revolution, and analyzes the Islamic Revolution and model of the Islamic Republic in terms of its relationship to the political milieu.

This study seeks to isolate and then analyze the dynamic, enduring cultural values and understandings that contribute to a particular political culture in Iran. In so doing, a clearer perspective of the Iranian political system, especially in terms of legitimacy, development, and change, is attained.

II

The Legacy of Authority in Iran

In a sense, a people's identity is shaped by history: the historical process involves individuals responding in a particular way to cope with their social experience. History unfolds as a people's inherited pictures of reality (ideas) meet with events in the world (situations), producing a particular outcome (response). Generally, new ideas may be created or old ideas transformed to fit a situation, but the national paradigm in which growth and development take place seems timeless and ongoing. Therefore, in studying Iranian history in terms of political culture, we can expect to identify prevalent national patterns and models that appear to define the parameters in which responses occur. We can see how ideas run through different situations and how they affect responses.

In examining the history of Iran, we are also looking at its politics. Frequently, patterns are based on individual rather than group politics. The history of Iran is marked by personalities and how they influenced the epoch in which they lived. Iran is a country shaped in part by authoritarian traditions. As we shall see, a key to maintaining political authority in Iran seems to be the ability to preserve the nation and culture from outside intrusion. Iran's history is one of foreign interference, and this aversion has apparently become part of the national will, an important political force in shaping Iranian history.

This look at Iranian history is an attempt to understand the sociopolitical experience of the Iranian people; in so doing, we can hope, in some measure, to identify the intrinsic paradigms in which the country functions politically. The period covered in this chapter begins with the nineteenth century, touching on earlier history as background to contemporary events, and ends with the consolidation of power by Mohammad Reza Pahlavi. The last chapter of the book gives full attention to the history and politics of the Islamic Republic, which is not covered here.

THE HISTORY AND SPIRIT OF IRANIAN POLITICS

For twenty-five centuries, Iran lived under monarchical rule. The greater part of Iran's recorded history, beginning circa 550 B.C., documents the rise and fall of greater and lesser monarchs. This chapter examines the primacy of the monarchical institution and the authoritarian tradition in Iran. The focus is also on antiauthoritarianism; on a nationalism that surfaced in the latter part of the nineteenth century, culminating in the Constitutional Revolution of 1905–9, and that emerged some forty years later into a revolutionary movement led by one of Iran's most noted nationalist symbols, Dr. Mohammad Mossadegh. For a twenty-year period (1921–41), Iran returned to the monarchical absolutism under the domination of Reza Shah.

The Constitutional Revolution of 1905–9 and the revolutionary events of the late 1940s and early 1950s are pivotal periods in Iran's history, setting the stage for future events. The motivational ideas behind the nationalist movement were in and of themselves not new to Iran, but reflected the antiauthoritarian character of Iranian political culture. In the latter part of the nineteenth century, with the penetration of outsiders into the affairs of Iran, distrust of arbitrary authority and xenophobia increased. What was especially significant about the twentieth century was its amalgamation of popular support, political power, and direct challenge to monarchical authority.

In these historical epochs, as in other important periods in Iran's history, ideas met with situations, and the responses are evidence of the paradigmatic patterns of the sociopolitical experience of the country.

MONARCHICAL AUTHORITY

Iran's history dates back some 2,500 years and can be divided into the pre-Islamic and Islamic periods. The pattern of events is generally the same, with greater or lesser figures in power, the forming of empires and dynasties, warring factions, encroachments and conquests—and the process is repeated again and again. Acceptance of authority in the political realm meant the dominance of a "strong leader," historically an autocratic monarch. Unrestricted by law, institutions, or tradition, the absolute power of the shahs extended as far as ambition, whim, or personal capacity permitted. Their autocratic rule encompassed every group and stratum of society. Because of the singular political authority of the monarch, the character of the individual occupying the throne has been of paramount significance to the fortunes of the state. The actions of an injudicious monarch generally resulted in political instability and loss of independence. The appellations for Iran's monarchs— King of Kings, Light of the Aryans, Shadow of God—hearkened to a time of great empire.

During its long history under various monarchs, Iran experienced periods of expansion and invasion. But despite the fact that Iran faced a new threat in the nineteenth century in European imperialism, the rhythm of monarchical authority continued. Although Western political and economic penetration was great during the Qajar dynasty, Iran escaped colonial status by playing the interests of one side against the other (for example, Russia in the north and Great Britain in the south). The principle of the absolute right of the monarch to everything in the land was not diminished by Western penetration, although the monarch's power in relation to the tribal chiefs and agents of the colonial powers was circumscribed. Although the Constitutional Movement was a reaction to British and Russian intervention and an attempt to mitigate the arbitrary and unwise use of power by the monarch, it was not directly aimed at abrogating the monarchical institution. It arose primarily out of discontent with inefficient governmental rule, opposition to foreign interference, and a fervent desire for independence from external forces.

In the coup d'état of 1921, Iranian history repeated itself: once more a strong leader appeared as the unifier of an enervated nation racked by civil war and foreign intrusion. One of Reza Shah's first goals was to centralize government control. He ruled as absolute monarch, extending state control over both the political and economic systems, until 1941, when the vicissitudes of war and Allied occupation led to Reza Shah's abdication to his son, Mohammad Reza Pahlavi. Reza Shah attempted to thrust Iran into the twentieth century through modernization, but there was no change in terms of the personalistic governmental norms and practices that had existed for centuries. The first real, and perhaps only, challenge to monarchical rule came in the early 1950s with the meteoric rise of an ardent nationalist, Mohammad Mossadegh. The power vacuum left by Reza Shah's abdication was filled through the political guile of this adroit statesman, with a long record in the Iranian Majlis. Ostensibly, the dominant issue of the time was Mossadegh's move to nationalize the Anglo-Iranian Oil Company (AIOC). However, the central issue was the monarch's place in the politics of Iran. The struggle for power was between a popular hero of the people, Mossadegh, and a politically weak Shah. But there was more at stake: the traditional autocratic system and patterns of government themselves were under fire.

FOREIGN INTERVENTION AND IRANIAN XENOPHOBIA: THE CONSTITUTIONAL ERA

Monarchical control went generally uncontested until the latter part of the nineteenth century, when the Qajar dynasty (1796–1925) found itself between two great powers contending for economic and political preeminence in Iran. In an involved struggle between England and Russia for hegemony in Iran, the embers of antiauthoritarianism and xenophobia were rekindled, dominating the national life of Iran and provoking some of the major confrontations to follow.

Prior to oil exploitation, it was Iran's strategic position and commercial routes within Asia that drew the predatory interests of outside powers—Genghis Khan, Alexander the Great, the Romans. The fact that Iran, unlike other Middle Eastern countries, tenaciously preserved its national identity throughout Arab occupation and the introduction of Islamic beliefs and that the invaders were gradually inducted into Iranian culture is evidence of the inherent rejection of foreign influence. Later Russia's expansionist policies on Iran's northern borders—plus Britain's policies of defending its colonial interests in India, controlling the Persian Gulf, and protecting its oil concession in the area—led to penetration by these powers into the political and economic life of the country. The map indicates Iran's strategic position in the Middle East

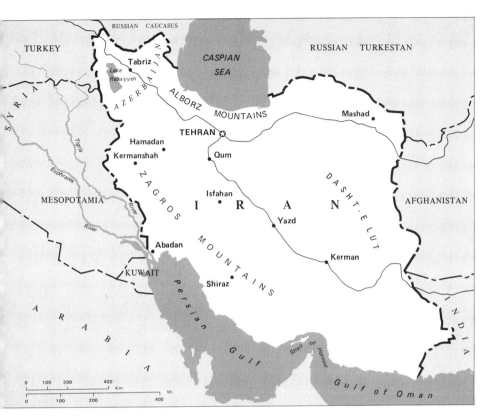

Iran's Strategic Position in the Nineteenth Century.
North: Russia borders on both sides of Caspian Sea.
South: Persian Gulf and Indian Ocean.
West: Turkey and Mesopotamia (now Iraq).
East: Afghanistan and India.

during the nineteenth century. Because of its location and natural resources, Iran has been directly affected by almost every important political event in the West since 1800.

Needing to finance their extravagances and finding themselves
caught between rival powers, the Qajar monarchs over a period of years
granted major concessions of large parts of Iranian territory, natural and
economic resources, and, ultimately, integral elements of national sovereignty to the rival colonial powers of Russia and Great Britain that dominated Asia at that time; these concessions left the country in severe
economic straits.[1] Although Iran was nominally independent at the

time, British and Russian influence was great. The foreign policy of the shahs was to pit the two imperial powers against each other in order to get what they wanted, usually loans to finance their excesses. The competing powers supported and manipulated the government of Iran through bribery and sundry pressures. In addition, Iran suffered defeat in two successive wars with Russia, resulting in the ignominious treaties of Gulistan in 1813 and Turkomanchai in 1828.[2] In 1838, Mohammad Shah attempted to restore the city of Herat in Afghanistan to Iranian sovereignty. War between Britain and Iran in 1838, and again in 1856, resulted from the British view that Afghanistan was a bulwark against a Russian drive toward India.

Two concessions had a profound impact on the course of events in Iran: the tobacco concession of 1890 and the oil concession of 1901. The tobacco concession granted the British was one more insult to the national sovereignty of Iran, and perhaps one of the precipitant factors leading to the Constitutional Revolution, the first occasion of united action by the Iranian people against the autocratic policies of the Shah and his court.[3] Tobacco was one of the few luxuries enjoyed by Iranians and one of their chief industries, and interference in this sensitive economic domain caused great restiveness. The people followed the lead of a prominent Ayatollah who issued a *fatwa* (edict) declaring tobacco use illegal and urging the people to abstain until the government repealed the concession. Merchants, most affected by the grant, petitioned the Shah to rescind the concession. The tobacco concession was abolished in 1892 because of popular pressure, and this had a marked effect on the participants: they realized that through unity and with the aid of their spiritual leaders they could influence the Shah and his court; and they became aware of the perils that reckless concessions to foreigners could produce for the political and economic viability of the country.

In 1901, Muzaffar al-Din Shah granted a concession to a British syndicate headed by William Knox D'Arcy to explore for and produce petroleum throughout the entire country, with the exception of five northern provinces adjacent to Russia. Oil was discovered in southwestern Iran in 1908; the Anglo-Iranian Oil Company evolved from this concession. Prior to the outbreak of World War I, the British government acquired a controlling interest in the company and thereby gained a resource that saw the Royal Navy through two world wars. As events unfolded, the AIOC proved to be an explosive political issue that galvanized national sentiments of xenophobia in Iran.

In the late nineteenth and early twentieth centuries, there was growing frustration, increased social awareness, and organization among urban groups because of the economic and political dominance by foreigners, an escalating financial crisis, and lack of reform. Iranian mistrust of power and foreign influence was intensified by what appeared to be collusion between the monarch and these unwelcome intruders, each seeking gain at the expense of the entire population.

Constitutional Era

Amid the fierce struggle between England and Russia for hegemony in Iran, the first movement against monarchical authority surfaced. These constitutional stirrings for independence were based more on a fear of foreign domination and a sense of injury than on any liberal theory or social philosophy. In his analysis of the role of the crowd in Iranian politics, Ervand Abrahamian points out that the Qajar dynasty had neither a standing army nor an extensive bureaucracy; its power stemmed from "the readiness of the magnates, the *ulama* (religious authorities), the judges, and the guild masters to enforce the Shah's will, and the disposition of the subjects to submit to his authority."[4] The misuse of power led to incredulity among certain members of the polity as to their continued obedience and submission to the Shah's will. The constitutionalists sought to curb the prerogatives of the Shah, particularly in economic matters, in order to secure complete independence from colonial control and economic deprivation.

At this pivotal point in Iran's history, attacks upon the traditional political system stemmed from the polity's outrage at the squandering of Iranian resources and fear of total domination by external powers. The monarch was not fulfilling the traditional role expected of him as a strong leader who protected the nation from foreign encroachment. The basis of monarchical authority was less secure than in the past. The dissatisfaction expressed during this period was not directed against the monarchical institution itself, but against the indiscretions of the individual occupying the seat of power.

The Constitutional Movement was essentially an urban campaign, with leadership and support coming from certain groups in the provincial capitals, particularly Tehran.[5] The combination of forces involved in the Constitutional Movement crystallized into three main groups—clerics, merchants, and intellectuals. Support among the vast majority of Iranians, who were politically inarticulate (peasants, tribespeople, and urban laborers), could only be elicited by a basic emotional appeal. The Constitutional Movement could not be considered a unified national movement. The actual revolution was bloodless, with merchants, mullahs, and students utilizing traditional methods such as *bast*,[6] agitations, and demonstrations. Among the preconditions laid down by the nationalists for their return to business and normal activity was the granting of a constitution and a national assembly. Because of the disruption of economic life and pressure from usually supportive groups, the Shah had little choice but to accede to the demands for a constitution. The National Assembly, composed of representatives from Tehran only, met for the first time on 7 October 1906.

The Majlis drafted a constitution, based on the Belgian model, which was ratified by the Shah on 30 December 1906, with Supplementary Fundamental Laws to the Constitution ratified on 8 October 1907.[7] The governmental model created transferred legislative power to a popular assembly, but the monarchical institution was retained, as well as the Shah's control over the army. Assembly delegates were to be elected from specific groups or classes, such as princes, mujtahids, members of the Qajar family, nobles, landowners, merchants, and members of the guilds. The principal concerns of the nationalists were reflected in the constitutional provision that reserved the power to regulate important economic matters, especially those involving foreign interests, to the Majlis. The principal goals of the nationalists were to eliminate foreign influence, to seek social reforms, and to check the tyranny of the Shah and his court. The constitutional provision (Article 48 added in 1949) that allowed the Shah to dissolve parliament at any time (new elections were to be called within a month of dissolution) demonstrated the embeddedness of the monarchical system in the political culture of Iran.

The makeup of the Majlis of 1906–7 suggested the religious and middle-class background of its members: approximately 40 percent of the representatives had such titles as Hajji or Sayyed affixed to their names, denoting the religious and social privilege of the middle class. Legislators were from the urban productive groups of bazaar merchants, skilled craftsmen, and guild members; peasants were excluded.[8]

The Constitutional Movement marked a period of concert and cooperation between the influential merchant class, who suffered directly from economic concessions and misrule; the ulama, whose power resided in the people; and the intellectuals, whose contacts with the West inspired many of the ideas that shaped the constitution. For the first time in their history, Iranians were asserting themselves overtly against traditional authoritarianism and against the Shah's capricious policies that acceded to foreign influence. Political power was temporarily transferred by the Constitutional Revolution, but it did not fundamentally alter the social or economic structure of the country.[9]

Defeat of Constitutional Government

Although the constitution provided a framework for constructing efficient and stable political organization, the events that followed reflected the tenuous foundation of the movement and the pervasive acquiescence to traditional authoritarian rule. Once immediate goals were satisfied, the Constitutional Movement lacked an ideological core on which to build political support and commitment. As E. A. Bayne remarks, "Protective nationalism is the principal theme of the Constitution rather than the promotion of popular democracy."[10] The ulama came to realize the secular threat to Islamic beliefs implicit within the constitution; once material demands were met, ideology would not sustain the merchants. There was no tradition of participation by intellectuals in politics, and they easily found their way back to engaging in parlor repartee. During the first fifteen years after adoption of the constitution, the Majlis met only for approximately three years. The constitutionalists found that constitutional government was inefficacious in a country long accustomed to authoritarian rule in which foreign interests had become firmly implanted.

The new government faced the interminable influence of the British and Russians, who were concerned that Iran might disturb the Anglo-Russian balance in the Middle East, particularly in view of the imminent challenge presented them by Imperial Germany. Subsequently, these two powers called a truce to Anglo-Russian rivalries over Iran by signing the Anglo-Russian Treaty in 1907, which divided Iran into respective spheres of influence—north and south—with a "neutral" zone in which either power was free to pursue its commercial interests.[11] In addition, the new government was threatened internally by a hostile monarch, Mohammad Ali Shah, who deeply resented the constitution. Aided by the Russians, the Shah made attempts to overthrow the Majlis by force, which led to his deposition in 1909. His twelve-year-old son assumed the throne.[12] Iran experienced approximately two and a half years of parliamentary rule, seeking foreign technical assistance from the United States. Between 1908 and 1914, tsarist troops repeatedly occupied the north and interfered in Iranian internal affairs.

The Second Majlis was confronted with a Russian ultimatum, supported by the British, to dismiss W. Morgan Shuster, a New York banker who had been hired by the Majlis as a technical adviser, and whose visible progress had buoyed the hopes of constitutionalists. While the cabinet accepted this ultimatum, the Majlis vehemently opposed capitulation to Russian demands. Subsequently, in December 1911, 12,000 Russian troops occupied the entire northern part of Iran, throwing the country into confusion and disorder. The cabinet staged a successful coup d'état against the Majlis. Nasir al-Mulk, regent for the young prince, became the principal political figure upon dissolution of the Majlis in 1911, with virtual power and control in the hands of Russia and Britain. "Besides partitioning Iran into spheres of influence and destroying the *Majlis*, the Anglo-Russian friendship induced an unprecedented degree of outright intervention in the affairs of the country."[13]

The Constitutional Revolution had failed to centralize government in Iran and build a stable financial or military base; instead, the British and Russians were more firmly in control than ever. The Majlis did not reconvene again until November 1914. The years following the Second Majlis up to World War I were characterized by insecurity and inactivity in Iranian government. During World War I, the government was in a position of subservience to foreigners, while maintaining a myth of neutrality.

In a letter dated 14 January 1918, written by Trotsky, the Bolshevik government in Russia declared to Iran the abrogation of all secret treaties between Great Britain and Russia and other powers that had violated the rights of Iran and disavowed all privileges of the tsarist government there.[14] While the Bolshevik government denounced the Anglo-Russian Treaty of 1907, British interference in Iranian affairs increased. The postwar years saw Iran in a deplorable state both administratively and financially. To ensure its interests in Iran and to restore control, the British government proposed the Anglo-Persian Treaty of 1919.[15] This treaty would have made Iran a virtual British protectorate and would have meant the loss of Iran's sovereignty, which had until then been at least formally recognized. Although the treaty was finally rejected by the Majlis, the debate on its ratification kept the government in turmoil for one and a half years. The agreement was intolerable to

Iranians, who resented the secrecy of the negotiations and the fact that they would be tendering their sovereign rights to Britain.

There are those who are of the opinion that Britain, once aware that Iran would not submit to satellite status, next sought to preserve power in Iran by supporting a more independent force in the country.[16] It was only a matter of time before Reza Khan and his Cossack brigade marched into Tehran (1921) and arrested the government. A soldier who had risen through the ranks, Reza Khan used the military to restore autocratic authority in Iran.

The nationalists had removed the monarch as head of the executive but failed to put something in his place. Iranian nationalists, accustomed to authority at the top, developed no coherent party system; neither did they produce a unifying figure who could capture the support of the polity. Reza Khan (later crowned Reza Shah) had no link with the revolution and did not identify with the constitution; he was above all a militarist and extreme nationalist.

The pendulum had swung from limited constitutional government back again to monarchical absolutism in the form of Reza Shah. For a period of some twenty years, Iran had taken a brief respite from monarchical rule by attempting a constitutional form of government. These were years of experimentation and confusion, stemming in part from inexperience and insecurity with the new governmental style. In addition, the revolution was thwarted at every turn by the inexorable intrusion of foreign powers. The phenomenon of xenophobia was reinforced in this period, as foreign penetration increased. The power and authority of the monarch had generally gone uncontested until the constitutional era. This may have been, in part, the result of the polity's perception of the monarch as protector of Iran's empire and independence to that point.

Although the monarchs of the Qajar dynasty fell short of the "strong leader" image of the traditional system, it appears that the great majority of Iranians were not quite ready to evolve the mechanisms needed to end the traditional patterns of government to which they were so long accustomed. The constitutional era seems to indicate the inability of the polity to create an evolutionary synthesis from propitious circumstances. Centuries of despotic rule and foreign invasion and domination created an environment in which individuals found it necessary to develop the means to frustrate the oppressor and protect their own interests. Inevitably, groups and organizations failed to evolve into an enduring political force, whereas individual skill and adaptability developed commensurate with the personal politics of the monarchical system. Political organization and unity were slow to mature and prosper in such a climate. Consequently, the autocratic ethic rather than the participatory ethic prevailed. By 1921, the country was ready for a strong leader to rule once again.

MONARCHICAL AUTHORITY: THE ERA OF REZA SHAH

The Constitutional Movement was an amalgamation of tradition and liberty. But with the ascent to power of Reza Shah in 1925, liberties were abrogated as he assumed total control over the processes of government in Iran. Reza Shah disregarded the constitution as he sought to modernize the country. Opposition to the Shah came from the emerging middle class and from the tradition-minded ulama, the group most directly affected by the Shah's secular modernization policies. Reza Shah's main support came from the bureaucracy and the army that he largely created.

From 1926 to 1941, Reza Shah ruled despotically; the government went from a weak constitutional monarchy to a strong, central bureaucracy, securing national unity by force. Although he did not annul the constitution, Reza Shah acted contrary to its spirit. The Majlis was the chosen and obedient instrument of his regime. His main goals at the outset were to subdue his chief rivals for power and to do away with any potential centers of opposition or revolt. This included the independent and influential ulama, tribes, the merchant class, and members of notable families. The centralist powers of Reza Shah became increasingly onerous as more and more groups were dispossessed. By the time of his abdication in 1941, Reza Shah was the largest landowner in the country. The arbitrary individual despotism of the past was replaced with the "organized omnipotence of the state."[17]

Reza Shah emphasized industrialization as a way to modernize Iran's economy. Roads and government-owned factories were built; the Trans-Iranian railway was completed in 1937. Secular reforms included such things as standardization and secularization of the school curriculum, the imposition of Western dress, and the founding of the University of Tehran in 1934. Reza Shah's aim was to free Iran completely from the interference and domination of various great powers who had plagued Iran in the past, and he used modernization as a means to that end. In the process of modernization, Reza Shah eschewed foreign loans entirely. Instead, the burden for his costly modernization efforts (the army, railway, and industrialization) fell entirely upon the people through taxation, which drained the country's wealth. While the peasants paid for the development projects, the Shah avoided increasing the tax burden of the landowning class. To secure revenue, he sold state-owned land to the landowners, thereby bringing tenant farmers directly under the landlords' control and also enhancing the landlords' economic status.[18] In his modernization policies, Reza Shah did not directly alter the traditional fabric of society. He obliquely affected the traditional and conservative elements of Iranian society, but the basic sociopolitical system went undisturbed for fear of undermining his stability and support. Prerogatives of the ulama were somewhat curtailed, but Shi'ite Islam itself was not attacked. The fact that Shi'ite Islam is closely tied to nationalism in Iran restricted attempts by Reza Shah to abolish it without endangering his position. Therefore, he attacked its modes of expression; for example, compulsory religious education was eliminated from primary and secondary schools. Dervish orders were banned, tazias suppressed, and religious property confiscated. In addition, little was done to reform the oppressive land tenure system or to pursue agricultural development. Rather than tackle onerous economic problems, it was safer politically to promote the economic symbols of modernity. A fitting example of the Shah's extravagant economic policy was construction of the Trans-Iranian railway, which had little economic justification since it was not needed for movement of any essential exports from the interior of Iran to the Persian Gulf.

Reza Shah thoroughly dominated the political process, building an omnipotent central government with himself and his family at the apex of the power structure. Despite some dramatic reforms, he was committed to preserving the traditional patterns of government by ruling absolutely and, later in his regime, ruthlessly. Bill and Leiden say of Reza Shah's regime: "It was within this repressive political climate that Reza Shah built a railway, founded a modern educational system, developed a national army, and supported such strong symbolic measures as the unveiling of women and the condemnation of the clerics. The old social structure and the traditional patrimonialism were strongly protected, however, by the new ruling Pahlavi family."[19]

During the 1920s and 1930s, Reza Shah was able to link himself with Iranian nationalism by defying the hegemony of the West and by standing firmly against foreign inducements and pressures. By stressing Iran's total independence from outsiders, he enhanced the xenophobic quality of Iranian nationalism. Paradoxically, the negativism inherent in this stance obstructed development of the positive stimulus needed for modernization at that time. Energy to mobilize support of the polity was directed externally rather than internally to accomplish needed reforms. This was particularly true among the beleaguered peasants; as one writer notes, "Only in the sense that independence from foreign influence meant independence of an Islamic country from the influence of non-Islamic powers could the peasant identify his interests with those of the government."[20]

Lacking was the ideological content necessary to provide legitimacy to the Shah's modernization program, which would have given popular identification to the governmental process, thereby closing the chasm between those imposing the reforms and those being imposed upon. Distrust of foreign influences provided the ideology by which the ruled could identify with the regime. During this period, governmental validity seemed based on the protection of Iranian independence. Reza Shah was a modernist but not a revolutionary in the social sense, for he left the hierarchical patterns of the sociopolitical system intact. "His charisma—in Iranian terms he was a 'strong man'—was related to his ability to protect the state."[21]

Reza Shah kept order in Iran for twenty years, but for most of those years the people lived as they had in the past under conditions of injustice, corruption, insecurity, and autocratic tyranny. "He did things to the people and for the people. Little was done by them."[22] Reza Shah's despotic regime fostered fear and insecurity, eliminating opposition and obviating the rise of new leadership. While developing surface manifestations of the twentieth century, his imperious and paternalistic policies did little to equip Iran with the properties of an independent state—that of a politically mature citizenry. Political rule as practiced by Reza Shah and his predecessors was detrimental to Iranian political development. Ruminating upon Reza Shah's reign, E. A. Bayne discerns that "Reza Shah's technique for ruling did not endear him to his people, who regarded him with fear mixed with awe. It did not build a lasting institutional structure because too few people were involved in fulfilling the functions of government, and for the same reason it did not develop a 'process of national will' conducive to further automatic political development."[23]

Reza Shah's Abdication

With the outbreak of World War II in 1939, Iran proclaimed its neutrality. The Iranian government received strongly worded messages from both the Soviets and the British (in 1940–41) to reduce the number of Germans in Iran. Iranian oil was important to the Allied cause. With the German invasion of Russia in June 1941, the most effective route for Western supplies to Russia lay through Iran. The Allies believed that Iran had to be brought into the war, and the presence of Germans in Iran offered the needed excuse. Knowing that neither Reza Shah nor the Iranian people would agree to such a move, Allied invasion troops occupied Iran after ultimatums were given to the Iranian government.[24] British and Russian troops jointly occupied Iran in 1941, for the expressed purpose of establishing a supply route across Iran to the embattled Russian army. The Allied invasion ignominiously crushed the Shah's army. Reza Shah, whose passion had been to secure permanent independence for Iran, refused to act as the nominal head of an occupied country and abdicated to his son, Mohammad Reza Pahlavi, in September 1941. Submission to Allied demands and responsibility for the consequences of occupation would have been incongruous with Reza Shah's nature and an abjuration of his life's goals. The inevitable conflict between the Shah and the occupation forces would have led to the same end. His insistence upon his rights would have meant the termination of his dynasty.

The events of 1941 came as a shock to Iranians as they faced dual feelings of freedom and insecurity that accompanied the departure of an autocratic ruler and government collapse, disintegration of the army, foreign occupation, and inflation. The national ego had been nourished during Reza Shah's administration, but his style of political rule and control left the country disorganized and unprepared for the larger social and political matters it would face.

From 1941 to 1946, the authority of the central government was circumscribed, as power was exercised by foreigners and a new monarch, the former preoccupied with their own affairs and the latter no more than a figurehead in Tehran. Restrictions limiting freedom of movement and speech that existed under Reza Shah were lifted. Political prisoners were freed, exiles returned, political groups formed, and newspapers and periodicals appeared; as one observer notes, "Barely two years after the abdication of Riza Shah . . . about fifteen parties and some 150 newspapers and periodicals had emerged on the political horizon of Tehran."[25] It was during the occupation that the thirteenth and fourteenth sessions of the Majlis met.

MONARCHICAL AUTHORITY CHALLENGED: POSTWAR IRAN

Power in Iran has been attributed to an individual not only as a result of ascribed status but also as a function of personality or charisma; this was the case in the next important epoch in Iran's history. Leonard Binder notes, "The monarchy is an institution, but the shah is an individual. The personality of the incumbent of the throne has an important bearing on the place the institution holds in the Iranian political system. . . ."[26] At no time would this be more true than in the postwar period. An anomalous national figure, in terms of the traditional political system, appeared on the Iranian political scene, Mohammad Mossadegh. As we shall see, the factor of personality in terms of political authority had a significant effect on events in postwar Iran.

From 1941 to the fall of Mossadegh in 1953, the Shah was just one more contender in the competition for power. The autocratic nature of his father's government left the young monarch with a tenuous base of support. Mohammad Reza Pahlavi had no creditable army to support him; the ulama, still cautious due to his father's secular policies, had not sanctioned the young Shah's ascent to the throne; the cabinet was not of his choosing; the Majlis was divided and acted independently; and new parties were springing up daily. Gradually, through compromise, the new monarch was able to win over sections of the military and the old aristocracy still tied to the traditional order; through concessions, he won over elements of the ulama. But the central government was by no means a strong body at this time, as cabinets headed by old-guard politicians rose and fell with frequency. The Shah's position, though clearly stated in the constitution, was politically unclear at the end of the war. Some factions were calling for the establishment of a republic; those in favor of the monarchy were simultaneously opposed to reinstatement of monarchical despotism in the style of Reza Shah.

In the intervening years, the crowd and public opinion became major elements in Iranian politics, with two organizations achieving the most success—the Tudeh (Masses) party and the National Front.

Party Politics 1941–53

With the war's end and the cessation of Anglo-Russian occupation, three broad political groups emerged: (1) the royalists, consisting of the Shah and his court, a number of army officers, large landlords and merchants, and other substantial elements of the country; (2) the left-of-center, Communist-oriented Tudeh party, composed of the disaffected of all classes, with its leadership and organization being dominated by the nascent, professional middle class; and (3) a heterogeneous collection of individuals and groups dissatisfied with the status quo, later to be known as the National Front. The opposition nationalist group in the Majlis, led by Mohammad Mossadegh, formed the nucleus of this movement.

The strength of the Tudeh party and the National Front in the late 1940s and early 1950s was such as to block the Shah in the Majlis and to challenge the very existence of the monarchy in 1953.

The Tudeh Party

The Tudeh party was aberrant in terms of Iranian politics, for it introduced new methods of organization. It was a party of ideas rather than personalities, with clearly defined social and economic goals. Among the reforms called for were a democratic constitution, land reform, schools, hospitals, and social security.[27] These were revolutionary goals in light of the entrenched authoritarian system that had existed for centuries, whose only platform was the desires and whims of the monarch. The Tudeh party was reputed to be a Communist organization, or at least a front. It attracted various classes of society: intellectuals, articulate trade-union members, and others who were not Communists or sympathizers, for example. The early success of the Tudeh party was evidenced by its representation of eight members in the Majlis in 1944, with three ministers in the cabinet by 1946.[28]

In February 1949, the Tudeh party was implicated in an attempt on the Shah's life and declared illegal by the government. But the underground network that developed after this episode brought discipline and solidarity to the party's rank-and-file. The party took a firm stand on nationalization of oil and against Great Britain as a venal intruder in the country. On the issue of expropriation of the Anglo-Iranian Oil Company (AIOC), the Tudeh party and the National Front found common ground.

The National Front

The National Front proved to be an amalgamating influence in Iranian politics. Its strong nationalism was spearheaded by one of Iran's most inscrutable national leaders, Mohammad Mossadegh. The National Front was successful in uniting disparate splinter groups calling themselves parties, which sought to influence specific segments of the population. These divergent parties were unable to formulate national programs responsive to the society as a whole. The National Front appealed to all Iranians and gathered popular support through a clear national objective. "The National Front succeeded in surmounting the ideological parochialism of the previous period by focusing the attention of all participants on the one task regarding which there was general consensus, i.e., the destruction of the British-Iranian oligarchy alliance which was perceived to be denying Iran independence and progress."[29] The National Front appealed to Iranian national sentiments by directing its ire at foreign interference, specifically the AIOC.

The unity achieved by the National Front was based partly on Iranian anger over exploitation of its oil resources, which aroused the inveterate nationalistic feelings of distrust and antiauthoritarianism not unlike those of the past, only more vociferous. The National Front consisted of such diverse strata of society as the Mujahedin Islam (Crusaders for Islam), university professors and students, and small merchants and businessmen, who resented foreign competition and ways. It was heterogeneous, embracing the religious and secular, upper class and peasant, Right and Left, but the nucleus of the party lay with the middle class. The National Front was a combination of the traditional *dowreh* system and a primitive party structure with a program that appealed to the national sentiments of the whole body politic. The dowreh system had played an important part in the Constitutional Movement in terms of mobilizing support and communications. This informal communications system linked the bazaar merchants from Tehran, Tabriz, and Isfahan with the ulama and tribespeople throughout the country. Literally, *dowreh* means circle; the word was used to describe upper- and middle-class groups that met regularly for reasons of common interest. The dowreh system was a surrogate for political parties and was used by Iranian politicians to discuss, organize, and transmit political information, ideas, and policies. The dowrehs and bazaars worked hand-in-hand. Bazaar merchants, who were dowreh members, in the course of business conveyed information and news to associates and customers. In the absence of an independent press, radio, or television, the dowreh system was the most effective means of communication between the elite and the populace as a whole.[30] This informal means of political communication proved significant in Iran's political future. Word spread through the mosques and bazaars that the National Front pledged Iranian independence and aligned itself with the ulama, giving a religious sanction to its brand of nationalism.

Among the religious exiles to return after Reza Shah's abdication was the politically powerful Ayatollah Kashani. As an elected member of the Majlis (1951), this very popular religious leader initially aligned himself on the side of the liberal nationalists and Dr. Mossadegh. Kashani had devoted his life to fighting the infidel British, and this was the primary basis for the alliance between Mossadegh and Kashani. Kashani's importance lay in his ability to arouse and control the lower middle class, peasants, and other generally apolitical groups. Kashani played a vital role, along with Mossadegh, in engineering the mass movement for nationalization of the AIOC.

The combined symbols of religion and xenophobia attracted the enthusiastic support of important sections of the society that otherwise might not have been included. Richard Cottam comments on the significance of nationalist appeal to the stability of Mossadegh's regime:

> From a control system perspective, probably few regimes in modern history have relied more completely on normative control. The symbols most successfully manipulated were those relating to Iranian nationalism. Mossadeq personally became a symbol of new found dignity for the ancient nation. . . . The belief was solidly held that British imperialism was the primary obstacle to any fundamental altering of Iranian society and must first be eliminated. . . .[31]

In the autumn of 1949, the National Front, led by Dr. Mossadegh, began its campaign for free elections and nationalization of the AIOC. Within a short time, Mossadegh had the support not only of a few politicians but—of more consequence—also of the masses. Mossadegh had defied the very roots of authoritarianism by challenging the Shah and disturbing the personalistic patterns of government in Iran.[32]

In 1951, Mossadegh submitted to the Majlis his proposal to nationalize Iran's oil by expropriating the Anglo-Iranian Oil Company. Riding a wave of public popularity, he was appointed prime minister in the same year by a reluctant and apprehensive Shah. He served as prime minister from May 1951 to August 1953.

There are those who praise Dr. Mossadegh: "It is no exaggeration to say that for the first time in Iran's very long history a national leader had appeared who enjoyed the respect, devotion, and loyalty of the vast majority of politically aware Iranians."[33] Mossadegh's appeal was not fortuitous, for he possessed certain characteristics that sprang from the Iranian social-cultural experience. For example, in Iran's patriarchal- and authoritarian-oriented society, Mossadegh, age seventy, fulfilled the people's inveterate desire for a paternal yet strong leader who espoused antiforeign sentiments. In a hierarchical system where familial status and land ownership placed an individual higher within the social sys- tem, Mossadegh was from an aristocratic, landowning family. In a coun- try with a long and persistent intellectual tradition, Mossadegh more than qualified as an erudite and educated man. He remained honest in a country deft in political mendacity; and his histrionics and sense of drama endeared him to a people accustomed to effusiveness. It was not uncommon for Mossadegh to become so emotionally worked up during an oration that he fainted. He brought to politics a brand of personal leadership that rapidly became a symbol of nationalism in Iran. Ironi- cally, one of Mossadegh's most serious problems while in office was an inability firmly to control the security forces; consequently, he was com- pelled to rely on his popular appeal for legitimacy. Conversely, the Shah, like his father, was unable to garner popular support and sought control through such coercive means as his personal domination of the army and the instruments of terror under his power.

In a short period, 1951–53, the monarch and court lost control over governmental activities; power emanated from a leader's popular- ity with the masses rather than from the legitimacy that comes from holding a traditional official position, with all of its coercive power. The force of personality and obdurate opposition to the AIOC—to foreign dominance in Iranian affairs—gave popular authority to Mossadegh's movement.

POPULAR LEGITIMACY: NATIONALISM AND POWER POLITICS OF THE 1950s

Two issues dominated Mossadegh's regime—nationalization of Iran's oil and the role the monarchy should play in the political system. The Anglo-Iranian Oil Company was an impregnable foreign enclave within Iran, employing many people and contributing a minimal royalty to the government. It was Mossadegh's conviction, shared by many in the Majlis, that public control of Iran's major industry was essential for the economic independence and modernization of their country. Oil revenues composed at best no more than 15 percent of the government's budget. Since the Iranian economy had benefited little in the past from this revenue, it was believed that it would not collapse if the royalties were reduced or eliminated. In addition, Iran watched as other countries moved to national independence (for example, Burma, India, and Pakistan) and as major industries in Britain were nationalized. Public opinion was aroused by figures published in the 1950s of the huge profits and benefits to Saudi Arabia and Kuwait from oil. In addition to wishing to benefit more equitably from their national resources and being concerned with conserving this valuable resource, Iranians were anxious to rid themselves of a foreign commercial and political influence.

Numerous exchanges between the Iranian government and the AIOC and Britain in efforts to solve the oil question only served to reinforce the inherent distrust and resentment of Iranians toward the AIOC, reaching the point of complete impasse in 1951.[34] Support for oil nationalization came from various strata of society, from portions of the aristocracy with animosity toward foreign intrusion, the bourgeoisie, skilled and unskilled labor, small property owners, religious leaders, intellectuals, students, and, in general, the middle class. Regarding the AIOC in Iran, one writer notes:

> The company was felt on all sides to be a baneful influence in the country. Its very presence was a source of corruption. . . . The company, and the British government behind it, welcomed stability; it was felt that they preferred to see the status quo maintained rather than a revolutionary upheaval that might bring about long-needed changes, but would inevitably interrupt the smooth commercial operation of the company. So it was to Britain's interest, it seemed, to keep the ruling clique in power as long as possible. . . .[35]

Among the resolutions received by the Majlis committee authorized to examine the question of an oil solution was that of Dr. Mossadegh and the National Front; the resolution read as follows: "In the name of the prosperity of the Persian nation and with a view to helping secure world peace, we, the undersigned, propose that the oil industry of Persia be declared as nationalised throughout all regions of the country without exception, that is to say, all operations for exploration, extraction and exploitation shall be in the hands of the government."[36]

It became apparent that nationalization was the only proposal that would receive approbation both inside and outside of the Majlis. With time, this volatile matter rapidly passed from the hands of government. Prime Minister Ali Razmara, an opponent of oil nationalization, was assassinated by a member of the radical religious group Fadayan-i Islam. The oil nationalization law passed in 1951. Over the opposition of the Shah, and at the request of the Majlis, Mossadegh became prime minister in the same year. Britain's failure to perceive that acceptance of the new law was important to Iranian self-respect and national sovereignty led to many of the problems experienced after passage of the oil nationalization bill. It appears that the Iranian government tried in many ways to work out an equitable and smooth transition; but intransigence and misunderstanding prevailed on both sides.

During this period no individual or group had the temerity to challenge Mossadegh. The young Shah, who favored a more circumspect policy on oil nationalization and who had the support of many loyal army officers, could have dismissed Mossadegh and dissolved parliament. But Mossadegh's popularity with the people precluded any such action. An American observer, present when the Shah appointed Mossadegh prime minister, was said to have quipped, "not satisfied with oil, the Majlis has gone on to nationalize the Shah."[37]

Ostensibly, oil nationalization was the focal point of political passions during Mossadegh's regime, but another issue of political importance centered around the Shah's place in the Iranian political system, the operation of the system, and the role of the army. Mossadegh's ambition was to eliminate the monarch and his army from politics.[38] Since the security forces were never firmly under his control, Mossadegh, adroit in Iranian politics, forced the hand of the opposition by direct appeals to the public, relying on demonstrations to bring opposing forces under his influence. In discussing the role of the crowd in Iranian politics, Abrahamian notes that "Mossadegh had come to power by the streets; he continued to remain in office similarly."[39]

Mossadegh's cogent use of the masses was demonstrated in July 1952. In order to deal more effectively with the economic problems of the country, Mossadegh made a request to the Majlis for full powers for a six-month period. At the urging of the army, the Shah refused his consent, since the request would have meant that Mossadegh would head the War Ministry. Mossadegh resigned, taking his appeal directly to the people. Tudeh party and National Front demonstrators took to the streets in often bloody demonstrations. Aware that popular support was with Mossadegh and that his position was tenuous, the Shah was pressured into asking for the resignation of his interim prime minister. The premiership was returned to Mossadegh and the full powers requested were conceded, including the Ministry of War. After assuming the post of minister of war, Mossadegh dismissed twenty-five generals and limited the power of the military courts. The Shah grew anxious as the prime minister's powers increased.

But once again foreign influence was to affect events in Iran. With the breakdown of oil negotiations in the summer of 1952, the American government moved toward the British viewpoint that Mossadegh was no longer a safeguard against communism—that the only alternative was a military coup d'état. The Shah and his supporters wanted Mossadegh out and were not adverse to seeking United States help in such an undertaking.[40] Anglo-American propaganda at the time dealt with the imminent Communist dangers in Iran and the importance of a stable monarchy.

Economic hardships resulting from Britain's blockade of Iranian oil as well as internal exigencies were factors in Mossadegh's eventual fall from grace. The continuing struggle over oil nationalization touched the large merchants, who felt the financial pinch from the loss of foreign exchange. The covert tensions and differences between Kashani, an ardent religious nationalist, and Mossadegh, a liberal nationalist, came to the surface in 1953 in an open split, with Mossadegh coming out on top. Kashani and his religious followers felt that Mossadegh was not uncompromising enough and might be tempted to make a deal with the British. However, the National Front coalition was weakened by Kashani's withdrawal of support. The royalists were quick to induct the malcontent Kashani into their ranks, as well as to enlist the support of Ayatollah Behbehani, who controlled a fairly extensive religiopolitical organization in southern Tehran.

Army loyalists were crucial in the overthrow of Mossadegh and the Shah's return to power in 1953. Prior to this, the army was caught between two loyalties—on one hand, to the traditional symbol of power, the Shah; on the other hand, to the national sentiments symbolized by Mossadegh.[41] By 1953, Mossadegh had gained a degree of control over the army from the Shah, through his position as minister of war. In July 1953, at Mossadegh's instigation, a national referendum on the dissolution of the Majlis was held, based on Mossadegh's contention that, as composed, the Majlis was an ineffectual body. The referendum held in early August gave Mossadegh a sweeping vote of confidence. On 12 August 1953, he announced his intent to dissolve the Majlis in conformity with the referendum, although this was strictly a royal prerogative. The Shah, confident of American support, reacted by dismissing Mossadegh and appointing General Zahedi in his place, then promptly fleeing the country. Mossadegh ignored the dismissal, arresting the officer who delivered it instead. The army, in conjunction with a mob well organized for the occasion (nonpartisan Iranians were paid by the Central Intelligence Agency for their participation), deposed Mossadegh after a series of riots. Mossadegh was arrested, and the Shah returned to power on 22 August 1953, after an absence of approximately one week. The CIA plan to overthrow the Mossadegh government was called Operation Ajax.[42]

There were a number of important cultural currents, in addition to other factors, that came into play at this point in Iran's history. Among these was the inherent Iranian distrust of power, as noted by one observer in 1965:

> This is not to say that Iranians distrust each other in all respects more than, say, do Americans, but that they distrust the possession and exercise of power more. . . . Where Americans tend to err on the side of idealism, Iranians tend to err on the side of cynicism. . . . It is rooted in reality, confirmed by reality, and, of course, shapes the reality of politics in Iran. . . . Iranians expect that the power of government will come to bear against them unless they can intercede with those who apply it.[43]

Iranian nationalism had emerged in reaction to a government supported and manipulated by competing foreign powers and what the nationalists felt was betrayal by the Shah and other powerful government officials. The belief that powerful foreigners and powerful Iranians working together were responsible for Iran's difficulties contributed much to the suspicion and distrust inherent in Iranian nationalism.

The new government of the CIA-backed Shah and General Zahedi did not escape the shadow of distrust and suspicion of the past, especially among the nationalists, who were convinced that American money and manipulation were responsible for their plight. The rapid influx of United States economic assistance to the Zahedi government, which was not forthcoming to Mossadegh in Iran's time of need, did little to allay their suspicions.

Part of Mossadegh's appeal and support came from his role as the weak David fighting the giant Goliath—the intrusive foreign powers.

When the British giant weakened over oil nationalization, and Mossadegh grew stronger, the underdog (the Shah) gained sympathetic support from some elements of society. Power is a fragile thread in Iranian politics. The paradox of at the same time respecting authority and power and rejecting it surfaced during this revolutionary period. Once stripped of power, Mossadegh could again be trusted; he became a national martyr, the symbol of Iranian nationalism. Mossadegh was a popular hero; but even at the zenith of his power, mass support was wanting when needed in August 1953.

As a political movement, Iranian nationalism reached its apogee during the period just described. Parties had never been stronger. The National Front and Tudeh party mobilized and involved more people in politics than ever before in Iran's long history. Parties of the Left, Right, and middle emerged. Mossadegh's attempts at social reform, free elections, land distribution, exclusion of foreign influence, and oil nationalization did not see fruition in his time, but their introduction would have a marked and lasting effect on political behavior and action in the future. Probably one of the most revolutionary developments of this era was the incorporation into the political system of an increasingly large and vociferous group—the new middle class—of increasing consequence in Iranian politics.

Political Perspectives—Mossadegh Era

The monarchical institution was severely threatened in the 1950s, largely because Mohammad Reza Pahlavi proved incapable at the outset of uniting nationalist sentiments behind him; instead these sentiments found expression through the National Front. During the 1920s and 1930s, the absolute role of Reza Shah was indisputable, and he embodied the traditional myth of a strong leader. He was able to monopolize national support because of his obdurate antiforeign feelings and his apparent ability to protect the nation. His fledgling son embodied none of these traditional symbols of Iranian nationalism; instead he appeared weak and uncertain. It was the charismatic Mossadegh who stood firmly for Iranian independence and against foreign interference in Iranian affairs, thereby winning the support of the populace, especially the burgeoning middle class. Mossadegh was not entirely out of step with the patriarchal ambience of Iranian political culture. To most Iranians, Mossadegh was a venerable and strong leader, one who staunchly supported the independence of Iran and would protect it from external threat. The Shah had a difficult time, because he had not established identification with nationalist sentiments from the beginning of his reign. Many felt the Shah was disloyal to the nation, because, as Huntington says, "In terms of support from his polity a monarch should aim to be dethroned by a foreign power rather than maintained by such powers."[44]

In terms of political development, the Mossadegh era represented in a sense a moving away from parochialism to a broader national unity. Parochial loyalties prevalent in a traditional society such as Iran were set aside by many Iranians, as Mossadegh came to represent the independence and dignity of the Iranian nation. Of most significance was the fact that his government was granted popular legitimacy by the polity, granted to no other Iranian regime before that time. This was the threat posed to the Shah and the institutional monarchy. The role played by the United States in ousting Mossadegh and the fact that the Shah benefited from that interference impeded his efforts at legitimizing his regime with many Iranians.

That the monarchical institution survived the challenge of the 1950s reflected its deep-rootedness in Iranian sociopolitical life. The security of a known quantity, in this case authoritarian rule, held sway over the polity, as Iranians faced the economic and political upheaval of 1953. As one writer said of the monarchy in 1962, "For most of the people of Iran it has always been there, and they cannot conceive of any other form of government."[45]

The proliferation of political parties during the period 1941–53 failed to bring Iran a stable parliamentary system. After centuries of authoritarian rule, it was doubtful that a parliamentary system of government would take hold in such a brief period of time. Iran's failure to achieve some lasting parliamentary principles may have been attributable to the role of the individual in terms of power. Power in Iran has been attained through ascribed status, or through one's place in society vis-à-vis the family, but it can also be a product of personality. Individual politics rather than group politics traditionally has been the norm in Iran. This was one of the difficulties confronting the Tudeh party; its emphasis was on group policy and it failed to produce a singular charismatic leader who appealed to the masses. The National Front reached a number of Iranians through the personality of Dr. Mossadegh, Iran's first really popular leader to espouse liberal, democratic ideas; many joined his camp because of his leadership. The emphasis on personal power relates to the monarchy as well. As history has shown, the personality of the individual occupying the throne had an influence on the role of the monarchical institution in the Iranian political system.

The resistance to fundamental change of traditional patterns of power and authority was evidenced by the maintenance of the monarchical institution in Iran for 2,500 years. Iran's political system of ruler-subject remained generally undisturbed until the twentieth century opened the area to new influences and pressures. The polity had learned to adapt to authoritarian rule, while maintaining a degree of individualism and national identity. Chapter 4 discusses how this was achieved.

The elaborate organizational apparatus that marked the administration of the Safavid dynasty was also a hallmark of the Pahlavi regime. In both, centralization was the goal: all functions emanated from the political leader, the Shah, who manipulated the system according to his own goals and desires. Bureaucracies, both civil and military, were merely extensions of the person of the leader. Personalism, informality, and balanced conflict dominated the system. The strategies of control included the creation of a strong loyal army; reduction of the powers of tribal leaders and the aristocracy; and control over the economic structure and consolidation of central administration. The ulama were controlled through co-optation into the system.

This was the nature of authoritarian rule in Iran during the twentieth century, but it was to undergo serious challenges in the same epoch. The events of this period reflect a subliminal movement toward breaking the yoke of traditional authority patterns that had dominated the political system of Iran from its early history. The Constitutional Movement was an initial step, though somewhat circumscribed, to separate the interwoven symbols of the Shah as government and as nation. The tacit assumption of the Constitutional Movement seemed to be that, as a constitutional monarch, the Shah would continue to symbolize the nation, but government would be in the hands of parliament.

From 1941 to 1953, the monarchical system underwent a serious challenge. During this period we see the infusion of new elements into the political process, such as popular support, political parties, and a developing and vocal middle class. In a country accustomed to authoritarian rule, this revolutionary experiment in popular politics at times appeared unruly, except for the stabilizing paternal symbol of Mossadegh. The dominant patterns of leadership embodying, along with the Shah, traditional interest groups (such as the old oligarchy, wealthy landowners, the military, and the clergy) combined with economic and political foreign interference were formidable forces against a control mechanism as volatile as popular appeal.

Mossadegh followed the lead of Iran's constitutional progenitors in attempting to segregate the monarch from governmental activities, but he appeared to be taking the country one step further. Although Mossadegh never called for the abrogation of the monarchy, his actions seemed to be aimed in that direction. By 1953, Mossadegh seemed more powerful than the Shah; his control reached to the Majlis, the military, and above all the public. What Mossadegh would have done with this power had he been allowed to continue in office and what the role of the Shah in the political system would have been remain speculative queries. But what was evident during this epoch in Iran's history was a diminution of the Shah's power and an incremental increase in the power of the prime minister.

Following Mossadegh's fall, the Shah moved to consolidate his power as leader of the entire country. His political tactics resembled those of his father, especially in terms of coercive control. In addition to strengthening the position and status of the army and gendarmerie, he organized an extensive secret police force. Mohammad Reza Pahlavi's first years as Shah were spent bargaining for survival. After a long period of maneuvering and balancing power, he was successful in reaffirming the traditional mechanisms of control, with himself at the apex of the power structure. Writing in 1974, Bill and Leiden noted that the Shah ". . . practices to perfection the techniques and tactics of patrimonialism that have traditionally prevailed in Islamic Iran. As a king who rules by emanation, he is presented as the source of all ideas and the fount of all good."[46] As the center of authority and power, the Shah maintained his control through the agents of coercion and reform, appealing to the power and material needs of the people. Any allowable change was commensurate with the preservation of the patterns of authority and control: any change in the sociopolitical system should strengthen rather than weaken the position of the monarch. The Shah and his court controlled the legislative branch of government and the security forces. Additionally, due to the symbiotic relationship between the economic elites and the governmental bureaucracy, based on mutual economic interests, the economic sector was quite dependent upon the traditional source of power.

The position of Mohammad Reza Pahlavi upon assuming the throne in 1941 was less than secure, but he moved from a position of total weakness to absolute strength, creating a central bureaucracy with himself in the seat of power and a political elite clustered around him. In a sociopolitical system imbued with centuries of autocratic and authoritarian rule, Mohammad Reza Pahlavi learned his lessons well. Due to its longevity and history, the monarchical institution acquired a legitimacy of its own. This legitimacy and the authority derived from it began to erode as Iran increasingly was trespassed by foreign powers eager to extract resources or to maintain position in the area and as Iran's monarchs failed to exercise authority in the interest of the nation.

SUMMARY

Iran differs from other Middle Eastern countries historically and culturally because throughout its long history of invasion and occupation, particularly in the Islamic era, it tenaciously preserved its national identity. Governmental authority was with the monarchs as long as they continued to protect Iranian independence and empire. When the monarch neglected his protector role and foreign encroachment increased, national pride as well as economic imperatives galvanized the polity to question governmental authority, which ultimately led to the constitution of 1906.

Identification with the state in Iran appears to have been more psychological than physical or legal. Government in Iran has been characterized by the power of individuals or groups of individuals (for example, the shahs and their courts, landlords, ulama, tribal leaders), not by the control that comes from written law in the Western sense. Laws governing Iranian society have generally been based on unwritten or traditional understandings or regulations. This centralization of arbitrary power in the hands of a select few led to a general distrust of power and insecurity within the polity. Despotic government, rule by personal authority and caprice, and the absence of prescribed laws and regulations to serve as guides to political action contributed to the chasm that existed between government and the people, and to the lack of political development.

Iranian history evinced the absence of trust and confidence in fellow political actors among the populace. These feelings had their roots in a precarious past wherein the privileged and powerful minority in Iranian society, particularly government officials, held sway over the majority of the people. Integration and group strength were stultified as individuals developed survival skills, which usually meant looking out for one's own interests and frustrating the oppressor whether a government official exacting taxes from a poor peasant or the Shah expropriating land from a wealthy landlord. The Constitutional Movement first awakened Iranians to the power they possessed if they acted together. The Shah's acquiescence to group pressure during the tobacco concession gave opposition groups an awareness of their nascent power as political participants. The nationalism of the 1950s was a politically integrative movement, for the first time joining disparate individuals and groups into a united front against the British monopoly in Iran and giving the people a sense of identity with the political system and perhaps with each other. These pivotal periods of public participation in the political process and confidence in political leaders were short-lived in contrast to the centuries-old system of authoritarian rule, but they set a precedent.

In terms of governmental output, history seems to indicate that the major expectation of the governed has been protection of the nation by its leaders from foreign encroachment and influence. Iranian literature and history tell of Iran's great past and the heroic deeds of its celebrated leaders (for example, Ferdowsi's *Shahnameh*).[47] Respect for political authority has been based on the ability of a strong leader to maintain Iran's national sovereignty and independence from outside forces; the Iranian leaders most admired were those who did just that. The general belief among the governed, based on a history of autocratic and often despotic rule, has been that government was an inimical force, against which it was necessary to be on the defensive.

The monarchical system of government precluded the involvement of nonelites in the governmental decision-making process. The pyramidal structure of government, with the Shah at the apex of power and elites of his choosing below him, meant that decisions were handed down to the polity; nonelite participation was limited to responding to decisions already handed down from above. This was generally the lesson of Iranian history. Prior to the Constitutional Movement, the devices used by those affected by monarchical decrees consisted of evasion, circumvention, temporizing, and the like.

During the constitutional era, the groups most affected by the plethora of foreign concessions responded by calling for a constitution and a parliament in order to curb the economic and political incompetence of the Qajar monarchs. For a brief period, input into the decision-making process was coming from a new force in Iranian politics—the parliament.

The revolutionary voices in the Majlis were eventually drowned out by the old-guard elite, and the role of this body in decision making declined. Postwar Iran of the 1940s and 1950s experienced a rebirth of political participation by nonelites as monarchical absolutism languished and nationalism thrived. This was a period of public demonstrations and participation by sundry individuals and groups; on the surface it often appeared chaotic, but it was salutary in a political system so long suppressed.

In terms of political culture, two themes appear to dominate in analyzing Iran's history: the long tradition of monarchical/individual authority and the strong feelings of independence and national sovereignty held by the polity. As presented in this chapter, these forces have been, at times, inconsonant, resulting in two important revolutionary and evolutionary epochs in Iranian political development.

The preceding pages have obliquely touched on the role of religion in influencing historical events and shaping ideas in Iran. In the following chapter, we shall take a closer look at the important relationship between politics and religion in Iran and analyze its special significance to Iranian political culture. Shi'ite Islam is historically intertwined with Iranian national identity and has been a vital element in the political, economic, and social life of the country. This relationship is the focus of the following chapter.

III

Religion and the Spirit of Iranian Politics

It is widely believed that the metaphysical dimensions of human existence give a particular character and form to the secular order of society and that the religious beliefs and understandings of the members of a society are essential in discerning their behavior vis-à-vis the political system. Although a religious system may undergo transformation or no longer appear to play a paramount role in a specific society, its after-effects are seen in the belief systems that develop and continue to influence social behavior. One example that readily comes to mind is the religiopolitical experience of the United States, founded in a puritan tradition, which in its many forms and stages contributed to the economic and political development of the West.[1]

Since a shared cosmology is a basic need of all cultures, it is an ingredient that cannot be eschewed in analyzing the political culture of a society. Throughout history, social conditions have led people to seek security and expression through various means, among them the spiritual. This is particularly true of Iran, whose past and present evince an omnipresent religious theology. Religion appears to have provided an answer to the helplessness and insecurity prevalent in Iranian society throughout its turbulent history and a vehicle for the expression of social and political dissatisfaction. From Iran's early beginnings, the Zoro-astrian religion was pervasive until the seventh century. With the Arab invasion, Islam replaced this ancient Iranian religion. With time, the philosophical and subtle Iranians adopted the Shi'ite heresy, perhaps to satisfy their need for poetry and romance. In addition, Iranian mysti-cism and speculative thinking fostered such social and religious theories as Sufism and the universalistic Bahaism.

It is clear that the national identity and consciousness of Iran are closely tied to religious beliefs. As one observer notes, "So important has spiritual devotion been in Iran that most of the social movements have had to appear in religious guise in order to gain the support of the submissive groups. The Persians' intense religious attitude has often been tapped as a source of invisible power. Traditionally, while the sub-missive group was bound to the dominant by force, its ties to religious authority were psychological in nature and appeared in various forms from Zoroaster to the Bab."[2]

The objective here is to pursue a more lucid understanding of Ira-nian political culture by analyzing the religious norms and values of the people, especially those of Islam, which has been the dominant religion of Iran for centuries. This chapter begins by analyzing some basic ideas and beliefs of Islam, then looks at the Islamic state and the schism that developed (based on the question of legitimate leadership from which Shi'ite Islam sprang), analyzing aspects of religion that have contributed to the creation of the distinct character of the Iranian state. We shall also explore the unique role and influence of the ulama in the Iranian political system, particularly in the twentieth century; how Iranians have responded to political realities through religious expression; and how re-ligious values have influenced political development in Iran.

DOCTRINAL AND LEGAL DIMENSIONS OF ISLAM

Islam is a monotheistic religion whose supreme deity is Allah and whose principal prophet and founder is Mohammad. Unlike Christian-ity, Islam has no formal organization: it is a continuum of action and a state of mind. There is no mediator between Allah and believers; Mus-lims' obligation is to God alone and not to any church. In addition, there is no institutionalized clergy in the Western sense. The external organization of Islam rests with a body of men called ulama, who are particularly learned in the intricacies of the faith. The religious authority enjoyed by the ulama is granted by the laity; leadership is based on learning and perceived morality.

Islam is founded upon the idea of an *umma* (community) of believers, equal before Allah and each other. Within the Islamic community, the rule of Allah is supreme, with unity and order flowing from him.

The most important sources of Islamic tradition are drawn primarily from the Quran,[3] considered by Muslims to be God's word revealed through his Prophet; through the Hadith, or oral lore attributed to the Prophet, which deals with points of law and religious dogma and practice; and the Sunna, or tradition associated with the Prophet's practices and actions. The Shari'a, or Divine Law, is the essence of Islamic religion, the law by which Muslims are to live. The principles of law contained in the Quran were explained and expanded in the Hadith and Sunna. The two most important sources of the Shari'a are the Quran and Hadith. The Divine Law of Islam guides Muslims in both private and social life. Only when individuals have accepted as binding the injunctions of the Shari'a can they call themselves Muslims. The prominence of legal concepts is paramount to Islam. The Quran is not only a source of law, but a guide to the practical life. It tries to integrate the political, economic, and social life of the Islamic community into a religious world view.

The Shari'a can be likened to immutable laws. Society's role is not to remake the law, but rather to "reform men and human society to conform to the law."[4] Consequently, man's role is not to construct laws, but to obey the laws revealed to the Prophet by God. In a political sense what follows from this construct is that the function of the political authority is to execute laws, not legislate them. In the Islamic view, God is the supreme legislator. The ulama, who are well versed in the law, are its custodians. By virtue of their scholarship in the Shari'a, the ulama are viewed as its legitimate judges and interpreters.

The Divine Law of Islam teaches respect for private property, while concomitantly opposing the concentration of wealth in the hands of a single individual. The Shari'a emphasizes the salience of the family to society and the dominant, patriarchal role of the father.[5]

The revealed law of the Quran took precedence over the law of the state in Iran prior to the drafting of the constitution in 1906–7. The impregnable position of Islamic law was evidenced when the drafters of the Supplementary Fundamental Laws of 1907 made provision for a

Board of Mujtahids to review laws legislated by the state as to their congruity with Islamic law. This was done to ensure that no law was passed that was contrary to the tenets of Shi'ite Islam.[6]

Article 91 of the Constitution of the Islamic Republic of Iran (1979) reasserted the dominance of Islamic law: "For the purpose of safeguarding the principles of Islam and the Constitution and to avoid any conflict between these principles and the laws of the Assembly, a Council of Guardians will be formed. . . ."[7] Six members of the clergy and six Muslim lawyers make up the twelve-member Council of Guardians, whose job is to oversee legislation as to conformity with Islamic law.

This overview of Islamic tenets was presented as a foundation for understanding the role of Islam in the development of political culture in Iran. We begin by examining the structure of the original Islamic state and the question of leadership, which eventually divided the Muslim community and gave shape to Shi'ite Islam, the dominant sect in Iran.

THE ISLAMIC STATE AND LEADERSHIP

By the time of his death, A.D. 632, Mohammad, through his confederation of tribes, was in control of much of Arabia.[8] Mohammad's prophetic message, which met with limited success in his native city of Mecca, was carried to Medina in A.D. 622. His *hijra* to Medina proved to be the beginning of a religious movement as well as a new body politic. Mohammad's sphere of influence spread not only through preaching and persuasion but through political and military means.

Although the community that emerged was characterized by a strong central authority, the original Muslim state was the corollary of Islamic religion. In Islamic perspective, the state exists through the will of Allah; its sole function is to enforce and preserve the Divine Law. Obedience to the state was considered equivalent to obeying Allah, but Allah's laws always superseded those of the state.[9] The political leader was expected to enforce and execute the laws of Allah revealed in the Quran. In Islamic theory, government is the handmaiden of religion: "The basic purpose of government is to give the community of Muslims internal and external security so that each may be able to gain a livelihood for himself and his dependents and to carry out his religious duties, especially that of worship."[10]

Among the enigmas surrounding the Prophet's death was his failure to name a successor or to prescribe a method for selecting one. Perhaps Mohammad did not formulate a policy of succession because he never claimed to be God's earthly ruler, but merely his messenger. This essential question of leadership following Mohammad's death was to cause bifurcation within the Islamic community, leading ultimately to two major divisions within Islam—the Sunni sect and the Shi'ite sect. The question of leadership after the Prophet's death is central to understanding the differences between Sunnism, the branch of Islam of the majority of Muslims, and Shi'ism, the branch most prevalent in Iran.

In the following pages we shall look briefly at the historical circumstances that led to the division within the Islamic community and the development of Shi'ite Islam. Although Sunni Islam has a larger number of devotees, Shi'ite Islam flourished in Iran and is an integral part of the society; as Seyyed Hossein Nasr writes, ". . . *Shi'ite* Islam has an intimate connection with the Persian soul."[11]

Schism within the Islamic Community

Sunni Islam, or orthodox Islam, is the religion practiced by the greater number of Muslims, while Shi'ite Islam constitutes about a fifth of the total Muslim population. Sunnism and Shi'ism spring from the same source. The major area of contention between them concerns the legitimacy of leadership following Mohammad's death.

After the death of the Prophet, the partisans of Ali, cousin and son-in-law of Mohammad, held that the caliphate (office of vice-regent), and the religious-political authority that went with the office, belonged rightly to Ali. Ali was married to the Prophet's daughter, Fatimah. According to Shi'ite belief, Ali's legitimate succession was based on his blood relationship and proximity to the Prophet. Ali's succession was also based on a promise Mohammad was said to have made that whoever would be the first to accept his invitation to embrace Islam and follow him would be his successor. Ali was, the story goes, the first to follow the Prophet's invocation and continued devoutly to do the same throughout the Prophet's lifetime.[12]

Following the normal Arab practice of calling a tribal council meeting after the death of a chief, the elders of the community met and elected Abu Bakr caliph and head of state. Abu Bakr was the Prophet's father-in-law and chief adviser for ten years. The minority who protested and refused to surrender to the majority in regard to Abu Bakr's succession, and who also held that this right belonged to Ali and the family of the Prophet, became known as Shi'ites, which literally means partisans or followers. A lack of sufficient political and military power as well as concern for the preservation of the Islamic community prevented open revolt against the existing political order on the part of Ali and his followers. The Shi'ites continued to maintain the belief that the caliphate rightly fell to Ali and his descendants, but held fast to the fundamental and external teachings of the Quran.

Intrinsically, consanguinity through the line of the Prophet became the basis for religious and political leadership within the Shi'ite community. Among the Sunnis, the caliph owed his position either to the choice of the community or to nomination by his predecessor.

Eventually, Ali assumed leadership as the fourth caliph of the Islamic community. But throughout this short term, his rule was bitterly contested. The Umayyad caliphate became firmly entrenched after Ali's assassination.[13] The struggle of those who sought to reassert the rights of Ali is the legend upon which much of Shi'ite Islam is built.

The Development of Ithna Ashari Shi'ism in Iran

For Shi'ites, the legitimate caliphate was vested in Ali and his two sons, Hassan and Hossein, and their progeny; because of this, the Umayyad caliphate and the Abbasid (successor to the Umayyads), which ruled for five centuries, were thought illegitimate. In Shi'ite Islam the only legitimate source of religious leadership and authority is with the sacred line of uncrowned caliphs, called Imams; Ali and his sons were the first three Imams. Ithna Ashari Shi'ism means belief in twelve Imams.[14] The Imamate began with Ali and was passed along through the eldest male offspring in his line, until its cessation with the last and twelfth Imam, Mohammad, called the Mahdi (the guided one). The Twelfth Imam is believed to have disappeared circa A.D. 874. It is believed the Mahdi will return from his hidden state (occultation) to rectify the evils of the world. Hossein (third Imam) is a key figure in Ithna Ashari Shi'ism as a symbol of goodness and justice. Various ceremonies commemorating his martyrdom developed and have taken on political significance in Iran, as described later in this study.

In the case of Iran, Shi'ism is a distinctive adaptation of Arab Islam to the culture of Iran. It seems the Iranians' tenacious sense of cultural independence from foreign intrusion and need for poetry and drama were reinforced by adhering to an unorthodox Islamic sect. Although loyal to Islam, Iranians resented their Arab conquerors, especially political rule from an Arab citadel far away. Shi'ism essentially mitigated Arab encroachment in the minds of the vanquished.

A link was established between Ithna Ashari Shi'ism and the Iranian monarchy through the belief that Hossein, son of Ali, married the daughter of Yazdgerd III, the last of the Sassanian monarchs of Iran, and that subsequent Imams were descendants of that union. In light of the cultural tenacity displayed by Iranians throughout a history of foreign encroachment, acceptance of Shi'ite Islam in Iran does not seem fortuitous or enigmatic; "a strong sense of being a unique and culturally superior people was instrumental in the Iranians' acceptance of the Shi- ite sect."[15]

Early Islamic history found Iran dominated by the Sunni form of Islam, with the Shi'ites generally a persecuted sect. But from the beginning, Shi'ism flourished in certain centers of Iran, such as Qum; Iranians generally revered the household of the Prophet. By the time of the Safavid dynasty, Shi'ism was rapidly gaining adherents in Iran.[16] In 1502, Shah Isma'il (of Sufi-Shi'ite antecedents) established Shi'ite Islam as the state religion of Iran, and unified the population in a common zeal for the Shi'ite faith.[17]

The discussion thus far has attempted to give readers an idea of the general beliefs and doctrines of Islam. We have briefly touched on the issue of legitimate rule of the Islamic community and the division it caused, leading to the Shi'ite sect. From this point we shall specifically analyze religion in terms of its significance to the Iranian political culture, identifying certain elements of Ithna Ashari Islam that have shaped the nature of the political process in Iran. To begin, however, it is necessary to step back in time from the importation of Islam to a religion much older in Iranian history and thinking: Zoroastrianism.

RELIGION AND THE IRANIAN STATE

Zoroastrianism and Political Authority

From Islamic history we see that religion preceded the state: Mohammad acted as a prophet long before he organized the Muslim community in Medina, and the state was founded for the sake of religion and not as a goal in and of itself. This was not the case in Iran, where it appears that the Achaemenian Empire prospered simultaneously with

Zoroastrian religion, with the state deriving divine sanction for its secular policy through religion.

Three great dynastic periods in Iranian history were intimately linked with religious history. During the first great epoch, the Achaemenian, Zoroastrianism was the national religion of Iran; during the Sassanian dynasty, Zoroastrianism experienced a renaissance and once again became the official state religion, remaining so until the demise of the Sassanian Empire. It was during the third epoch of the Safavid dynasty that Shi'ite Islam became the official religion of Iran. The religious character of the Iranian state is linked to its very origins.

The Avesta, the sacred book of Zoroastrianism, is both a religious document of Iran's early history and a basic source for the study of Iranian languages. Zoroaster's teachings centered on the interminable conflict between good and evil, with good prevailing over evil. The god of goodness and eternal light was represented by Ahura Mazda. Ancient Iranians were called upon to fight against the power of evil, or infinite darkness, represented by Ahriman or satan. Articles of faith included belief in the immortality of the soul, freedom of will, the last judgment, an angelic world, and the sacredness of human life.[18]

This ancient religion is important because of its progenitive nature and imprint on the major religions that followed it and because of its effect upon and interaction with the political system of Iran. Church and state were one during the Achaemenian and Sassanian dynasties of ancient Iran. The Sassanian monarchs left behind inscriptions and sculptures depicting themselves as receiving the throne by divine right direct from Ahura Mazda.[19] The political philosophy that emerged from Zoroastrianism upheld the supremacy of the monarch.[20] As we shall see, the ideas of monarchical supremacy and divine right were carried over, with some modification, to Iranian Shi'ism. The case for absolute and hereditary monarchy was made early in Iranian history within religious dimensions. Concerning Zoroastrianism and its relevance to the development of political thinking in Iran, R. C. Zaehner has noted, "This near-identity of Church and State which the Zoroastrians themselves admitted had been fatal to their religion once the Iranian monarchy collapsed, was nevertheless firmly embedded in their thought."[21]

Iranian perceptions of monarchical absolutism seem to emanate from two ideas of authority, one that relates to ancient Iran and Zoroastrian doctrine and the other based on Shi'ite Islamic theology. The near-identity of political and religious authority during Iran's early history and the promulgation of the idea of a quasi-divine monarchical rule were perceptions that influenced Shi'ite Islamic thinking in Iran. The Arab invasion and the triumph of Islam in the seventh century A.D. saw the overthrow of the Sassanian dynasty and the demise of Zoroastrianism as the religious creed of Iran.

Ithna Ashari Shi'ite Islam and Political Authority

From its inception, Shi'ite Islam differed from orthodox Islam regarding the question of legitimate succession after the Prophet's death. Leadership, in the form of the caliphate, was nowhere mentioned in the Quran or in Prophetic instruction, but was based on social necessity. Although both sects trace their origin to the religious mission of the Prophet, Shi'ism's roots are firmly set in the political questions of leadership and authority; it was in origin a political movement. The history of Shi'ite Islam deals with the rise and fall of various leaders.

The Imamate. The term *Imam* varied among orthodox Muslims and Shi'ites. For the Sunni, it meant the chosen leader of the faithful, both in religious affairs and as defender and administrator of the Muslim community. But for Shi'ites, it meant Ali and his eleven successors, who possessed divinely inspired truth and knowledge. Shi'ite Imams were distinguished (having no parallel in Sunni Islam) by intercessionary powers stemming from their suffering and martyrdom and by their qualities of sinlessness and infallibility. Shi'ite Islam is a religion of authority. Shi'ites believe that the messianic knowledge and legitimacy of Ali were transferred to each Imam without interruption. Ali and his sons, Hassan and Hossein, and the Mahdi have special meaning and importance in Ithna Ashari Shi'ism.

Shi'ites believe, as do the Sunnis, that "there is no God but Allah, and that Mohammad is the apostle of God," but to this the Shi'ites added the notion that Ali is the Vali al Allah (vice-regent of God). Ali's esteem in Shi'ite Islam often appears to equal that of Mohammad, although this would not be readily admitted.[22] The martyrdom of Hossein (he and a number of followers were massacred by Sunnis at Karbala) has been the focus of elaborate ceremonies during the month of Muharram for centuries in Iran. In these ceremonies, Iranians vicariously identify with the martyrdom and suffering of Hossein and with his efforts to overcome venality and injustice.

There is an intimate relationship between the Imamate and Iranian political authority. The Shi'ite head of state was referred to as Imam rather than as caliph; and according to Shi'ite doctrine, all power, spiritual as well as secular, was vested in the Holy Imam. In this sense, all political authority lacks legitimacy in the absence of the Imam. Four aspects of Ithna Ashari Shi'ism, dealing with the leadership and authority of the Imamate, set it apart from orthodox Islam and appear to have contributed to the political patterns that developed in Iran: (1) the duality and correlation of the sacred and temporal; (2) its authoritarian nature; (3) its elitist and hierarchical character; and (4) the messianic nature of the Twelfth Imam.

In keeping with orthodox Islam, Shi'ites adhere to the doctrine that Mohammad was the last of the prophets and that his revelation was a perfection of earlier ones; therefore, the Imam is not thought of as a prophet. It is in terms of the function and nature of the Imam that disagreement occurs. For Sunni Muslims, the sovereign's authority was derivative, and ultimate power remained Allah's; the authority of the caliph was circumscribed by the Shari'a. Sunnis considered Mohammad's successor to be caliph only, with the primary function of protecting the religious community. Conversely, for Shi'ite Muslims, the Imam's function was to interpret Quranic law and to develop, apply, or enforce it as new situations arose. As a source of instruction and guidance, the Imam was unequivocal, infallible, and absolute, since he was thought to rule by God's will and in his name. Loyalty to the Imam as leader of Shi'ite Muslims was based on the belief that Ali had inherited from the Prophet both his spiritual and secular authority and that those powers were passed unbroken to each Imam thereafter. In Sunni Islam, the primary attachment was to a program, namely the Quran and the Hadiths. The basic attachment of Shi'ism was to a person, the Imam, thought of as a divinely inspired leader most capable of properly guiding the faithful. Contrary to Sunni theology, in Shi'ism, the Imam is viewed as the legitimate ecclesiastical and temporal ruler.

The head of the Shi'ite community was essentially an autocratic ruler, in that the Imam's legitimacy and authority stemmed not from election by the people, but from the prerogative of divine right passed to him by his predecessor. The authority of the Imam sprang not from the people, but rather from his role as the representative of God. This led to the assumption that the community would follow and accept his decisions and the totality of the Shi'ite religious system.

According to Shiʿite doctrine, the Imamate is hereditary. Shiʿites believe that members of the Hashim clan (family of Mohammad) had special powers that distinguished them and set them above others. From this hereditary network developed a form of elitism in which a select group was regarded as the ultimate authority, the source of truth, and the only beings worthy of obedience.

The Twelfth and last Imam is believed to be present in every age, but hidden until the day of his second coming as Mahdi to restore justice and righteousness in the world. After the disappearance of the Mahdi, a collective body of mujtahids exercised the prerogatives of his office, while awaiting his expected return. The tradition was significant in establishing the authority and esteem of the ulama in Iran. The messianic idea of the Mahdi is an important principle in Ithna Ashari Shiʿism, but not in Sunnism. The idea of a savior is natural to a people who historically experienced social and political suppression. Inherent in the idea of the Mahdi is the feeling of oppression, discontent, and hope for change with the return of the saintly Imam. Identification with a minority body, deprived of rights, was relatively easy for Iranians, who saw their nation vanquished by the Muslim majority; identification with the idea of the Mahdi seemed to fit with the monarchical political system of Iran.

The Imamate and the Iranian Monarchy. The importation of Islam to Iran did not seem to abrogate the ancient pattern of affinity between the monarch and religion, but rather was assimilated into Iranian sociopolitical traditions. The correlation of religious and political authority appears to have been influenced by the concept of the divine right of kings of pre-Islamic Iran, wherein Zoroastrianism and dynastic authority were closely linked. The traditional authoritarian relationship between a strong leader and willing, or unwilling, followers seems evident in Iranian Shiʿism, specifically in its distinctive belief in a powerful, charismatic leader. The historic patrimonialism of Iran found expression in the Shiʿite belief that salutary effects result from following and obeying a charismatic leader of "the family." As one writer remarks, "Shiʿism shows the deep desire and indeed yearning of many Muslims for a divinely guided leader."[23]

The interrelationship of religion and politics in Iranian Shiʿism provided a propitious environment for political leaders to link themselves to divine authority. Shiʿite Muslims developed a distinct political-religious community in Iran, an intricate system in which submission to religion often also meant submission to Iranian political authority, and vice versa.

The belief developed within Shi'ite doctrine that the mujtahids were to represent the Hidden Imam until his reappearance, his being the only legitimate authority. Iranian monarchs traditionally attempted to legitimize their authority by linking themselves with the Imams and religion in general. Historically, the assumption was that the religious order had indefinitely delegated certain of its temporal prerogatives to the political authority in order to protect the theocratic social order and religious interests in society. Ultimately, this symbolic delegation of authority from the religious to the political provided the monarchs with a unique moral position and authority. Regarding government of the Ithna Ashari Shi'ite state, theory held that a pious and powerful leader, guided and advised by the "general agency" (a body of Shi'ite mujtahids) of the Imam, would rule in absentia until the Hidden Imam returned. According to Ithna Ashari Shi'ism, all government is imperfect in the absence of the Mahdi; under these circumstances, the best form of government was a monarchical system that ruled with the consent of the ulama.

The bond between religion and the state was reinforced in the sixteenth century by the Safavid dynasty when it established Shi'ite Islam as the official state religion. Through this accommodation, a trade-off was struck wherein the state gave political recognition to the Imamate and a kind of religious legitimacy was bestowed upon the political authority, the Shah. Because Shi'ite Islam was the official religion of the state, the ulama tended to acquiesce to monarchical authority. But the temporal authority of the Imam was never relinquished.[24] In effect, this action by the Safavid state established the notion of loyalty to Iranian political authority until the return of the Mahdi. As guarantor of the Shi'ite community, the role of the monarch was to foster the general good, thereby advancing the faith. The close association of the political and religious added to the authority of the monarchy.

The autocratic nature of Shi'ite doctrine was not aberrant from pre-Islamic conceptions of monarchical rule, from which sprang such monarchical appellations as Shadow of God and other equally grandiose titles. "Shi'ite doctrine was partly drawn from an ancient absolutist past in Iran, a reflection of the patrimonial origins of the kingdom and the political exigency of Safavid efforts to unify a divided empire."[25]

The acquisition of religious legitimacy by the political authority essentially meant de facto, if not de jure, delegation of legitimacy to the Shah himself, since Iran has historically been an absolute and autocratic state. The Shah, because of this, theoretically assumed the role not only of defender of the Iranian state but also of trustee and defender of the Shiʿite community.

The political implications of such a dual authority base were especially significant to the political system of Iran, particularly in buttressing the monarchical institution, whose secular power was already absolute. Implicit in the relationship between the Imamate and the monarch is the aspect of superiority over commoners. The idea of the Shah's possession of superior political wisdom and virtue not only gave further support to the hierarchical system in Iran but also ruled out for the time the probability of popular dissent. As defender of the religious community in the Imam's absence, the monarch could demand the same loyalty from his subjects as would the Hidden Imam, should he reappear. Concomitantly, the interregnum status of the monarchy in the Mahdi's absence tinged it with a degree of uncertainty. If the monarch failed to defend the faith and community, however that might be interpreted, or attempted to usurp the authority of the Imamate, then his authority could be challenged. This was the case during the constitutional era, the 1950s, and the Islamic Revolution of 1978–79.

Correlation between Shiʿism and Secular Order and Its Meaning to the Political System

The indivisibility of the religious order from the political order in Iranian society had important ramifications in terms of how the people viewed their role and behavior within the political system. The difficulty of separating the religious from the political created a tension when one or the other came under attack. The underlying belief that social and political disintegration might perhaps follow dissolution of the monarchy seemed prevalent in Iranian society prior to the Constitutional Revolution of 1905–9. In the 1920s, when Reza Khan considered a republican form of government in Iran, the most vociferous opposition came from religious leaders, who exerted sufficient pressure to preserve the traditional system. As seen in chapter 2, even during the Constitutional Revolution, the monarchical institution itself was not directly under attack; rather, the focus was upon government mismanagement, venality, and tyranny that were undermining the security of the state.

The period of the 1950s in Iran is a striking example of the societal tension created by a challenge to political authority. During the last turbulent days of Mossadegh's government, the polity was not totally amenable or ready to discard the traditional rule of the monarch. Religious and political identity with the state, represented by the monarchy, was certainly a factor in the political denouement of the 1950s. During that volatile period, Iranians were confronted with a situation in which, to effect change, a rethinking of their religious, political, and total beliefs would have been required. More time would be needed for such rethinking. The authority of the monarch, based on protection of the Shi-ʿite community, was challenged in the late 1970s. External Western influences were perceived as eroding Iranian traditions, culture, and spiritual values. This was one important factor in the Revolution that brought down the monarchy and brought up a new political order based on rule by the religious order. The survival of the monarchy for 2,500 years in Iran was largely due to the long-standing bond between the religious and secular order. As one writer states, "Shiʿa not only is a national religious expression, . . . but it may also be regarded as the religious identity of the Iranian nation."[26]

The historic patrimonial hierarchy that characterized the Iranian political system was an efficacious system for the incorporation of Shiʿite Islamic religion, with its emphasis on elitism and religious hierarchy. The original community of Muslims in Medina was a patrimonially structured system with the Prophet as the absolute and special leader. Shiʿite Islam preserved this hierarchy by claiming the divine right of special leadership for Ali and his descendants. The monarchical system of government in Iran was fertile ground for the religious hierarchical and hereditary order of Shiʿite Islam.

Iran differs from other Middle Eastern countries in that it was able to maintain its national identity throughout its many invasions, including the Islamic incursion. As we saw in chapter 2, a large part of Iranian national identity revolved around a universalistic idea of Iran's great past and civilization based on monarchical rule. This national identity was an important factor in the development of Ithna Ashari Shiʿite Islam in Iran. It is interesting that in other Muslim states we see some experimentation in governmental forms as compared to the monarchical absolutism of the Iranian state up to the twentieth century. The reasons for this require prolonged research. Briefly, we know that the Prophet was absolute ruler of the Islamic community and that he left no instructions as to what form of government the Islamic state should adopt and who should assume leadership after his death. In orthodox Islam, the political and religious absolutism of the Prophet was not passed to his successor. Abu Bakr and his successors assumed leadership of the Muslim community to protect the religious order, but theirs was a purely temporal rule. Mohammad's effectiveness stemmed from his absolute legitimacy as leader in a religious sense; this did not apply to the caliphs who followed him. In addition to the dissipation of absolutism in Sunni Islam, the fact that Mohammad left no definitive indications of state organization allowed the Sunni community the freedom to contemplate and experiment with different ways of governing. This was not the case with Shi'ism, in that the Imams were believed to be endowed with absolute religious as well as political power. The hierarchical and hereditary bias of Shi'ite Islam and its belief in the divine right of the ruler essentially defined the type of government that would be congruent with its credo. The orthodoxy of Shi'ism ultimately dictated political expression. Nowhere was this more evident than in Iran, where traditional governmental absolutism combined with the religious absolutism of Shi'ite Islam.

Another aspect of the Iranian experience marks its distinction from the political experience of orthodox Muslims. For Arab Muslims, history begins with Mohammad and the establishment of the Islamic community.[27] No similar notion exists among Iranian Muslims, who for centuries have extolled the bravery and courage of Iran's ancient rulers such as Cyrus, Darius, and Xerxes, and who have derived a sense of national pride from a glorious past and heroic leaders. As one writer remarks, "If the Persian monarchy had been closer to the spirit of orthodox Islam and had drawn its raison d'être solely from Islam rather than from non-Islamic, national sources, constitutionalism and secularism would have greatly undermined its strength."[28]

At this point, it is especially important to comment on the indigenous independence of the Iranian people, so that readers do not get the mistaken impression that Iranians blindly follow political authority. The adoption of Shi'ism at the beginning of the sixteenth century as the official religion of Iran was important in terms of nationalism; but unlike Sunni Muslims, Iranian Muslims derive their national identity from a history of centuries of independent rule and empire.

Various Iranian traditions contribute to the people's sense of national independence. Although the religious institution was often in line with the establishment, it has always preserved its independence and proven to be a source of contention for the political authority. Centuries of absolute monarchical rule created a situation in which obedience to authority was necessary for survival, but this did not eliminate cynicism toward political authority or the oft-noted adroitness at circumvention, or Hajji-Babaness, that has characterized the inhabitants of Iran.[29]

The seeds of Shi'ite protest and opposition in Iran can be seen in the centuries of experience as a minority faith, with its history of persecution, tragedy, and martyrdom. The representation of Imam Hossein, who according to Shi'ite tradition was slain while on his way to reclaim leadership of the Islamic community, as a symbol of action against oppression and injustice has given an independent zeal to Ithna Ashari Shi'ism in Iran. Shi'ism was born in rebellion and reflects a recalcitrant attitude toward secular authority. Shi'ites refused to grant legitimacy to any government after the Prophet's death other than that of the first Imam, Ali. An essential obligation of the Shi'ite faith is the doctrine of obedience to the rule of the Imam. With the disappearance of the Twelfth Imam, continuity with the rule of the Imam passed to the authoritative interpreters of the religious laws, the highest-ranking ulama. Another aspect of Ithna Ashari Shi'ism important to the Iranians' perspective on political authority is the belief in the return of the Mahdi to establish justice and order in the world. Inherent in this belief is the notion of the imperfection of society and the temporal political authority. All of these factors have created conflict at times between the state and the religious order in Iran.

The parallels between the authoritarian, elite, and hierarchical character of Shi'ite Islam and the nature of Iranian government are apparent. Also, the interrelationship of religion and political authority is an influential factor in how the ulama and their followers responded politically during pivotal historical periods. The following section analyzes some of those responses. The principal aim is to analyze the role and influence of the religious order on the functioning of the Iranian political system.

ROLE AND INFLUENCE OF THE RELIGIOUS ORDER IN THE IRANIAN POLITICAL PROCESS

The interconnection between the religious structure of Ithna Ashari Shi'ism and the political authority gives a religious tone to political life in Iran. Shi'ism was ultimately shifted from its strictly Islamic base and linked with the historical tradition of Iran. The Iranian political system prior to the Islamic Revolution was primarily a traditional system, whose main pillars were "a divine-right king, an aristocracy legitimized in a parliament, and an established religious institution."[30]

Like culture in general, Iranian culture developed as an answer to the life situation. The exigencies of a history replete with dominance, of both an external and internal nature, prompted Iranians to seek solutions to their helplessness and insecurity in various protective mechanisms. Religion provided one such answer to the human condition.

Autonomy of the Iranian Religious Institution

There are in Islam no priests or ministers in the Western sense of the word. Men who are recognized as particularly learned in Islamic doctrine are known collectively as ulama. Authority and advancement are based upon knowledge and conduct. The ulama are not a monolithic group; neither are they hierarchically organized. Since the ulama are drawn from all ranks of society, they cannot be considered a caste. In the past, religious service (and military service) offered the best opportunity for mobility in Iran. Regarded neither as priests nor as mediators in a ritualistic sense, their role was to provide divine guidance to the Shi'ite faithful in the absence of the Hidden Imam, and they derived a special legitimacy from this role. The Iranian Shi'ite ulama are either mujtahids, who are scholars trained in religious colleges, versed in interpreting religious law for the community, or mullahs, whose education is briefer and whose duties include preaching in mosques, giving religious instruction in *maktab*s (religious schools), and performing the religious duties of daily life. A mujtahid takes the honorific title of ayatollah (reflection of God) when he has reached the apogee of spiritual development and has demonstrated the capacity to attract followers and express their desires.

The trusteeship that Shi'ite Islam placed in the hands of the mujtahids created an unending tension between the secular power (the shahs) and the religious power. The religious leaders, because of their close relationships with their followers and their reputations for veracity, became the conduits and, at times, organizers of public protest against the repression and venality of the regime. Believers are in a sense bound to follow the guidance of the Imam. The community is divided into those who make judgments (the mujtahids) and those who must accept the judgments of others (*muqallid*). The mujtahids may claim no infallibility; their opinions and rulings vary. The faithful are not obliged to accept their pronouncements. At the same time, to guarantee some continuity of authority it is obligatory for Shi'ites to follow the direction of a certain mujtahid.[31]

The ulama have played a paramount role in the Iranian sociopolitical process. In earlier times, religious leaders wielded great influence through their control of the Iranian legal and educational systems. In addition, their extensive lines of communication with government and, more important, with the people have been a continuing source of influence. This direct communication was a potent force in the sociopolitical motivation of the masses during pivotal historical periods of Iran's recent past. On a number of occasions, the ulama used the power of their position to challenge the regime: for example, during the Shah's land reform program and the ultimate challenge, the Islamic Revolution of 1978–79. The political power of the ulama rests with their influence over a large majority of the population, the peasants and lower urban classes. Because of their prestige and popularity, the ulama at times acted as a pressure group through their access to and leverage with the political authority. Historically, the ulama have taken the side of the individual or group that affirmed the traditional position of Shi'ite Islam as the state religion of Iran and that insisted upon national independence and, obliquely, the independence of the Shi'ite clergy from political intrusion. Generally, in the past the ulama reacted ambiguously to the political authority, supporting or opposing governmental policies based on the autocracy of the regime and its policies vis-à-vis the position of the ulama. The Shi'ite ulama have not been challenged in their religious authority in the manner that the Sunni ulama have. Even the religious reforms of Reza Shah, thought drastic by Iranians, in no manner approximated those of Kemal Atatürk, whose reforms undermined the very structure of religion and culture in Turkey.

The sociopolitical structure of pre-Islamic Iran was based on the absolute authority of the monarch and court, which was supported by a powerful clergy, military, and bureaucracy. During the Islamic epoch, the Safavids reestablished the dynastic authority and traditions of the past, with the ulama supporting the monarchical system. Before World War I, the ulama were one of the most independent nongovernmental centers of power in Iran because they controlled their own wealth, education, and legal system and were respected by the people.[32]

Iran's monarchs were cognizant of the value of preserving the link between government and Shi'ite Islam as a means of maintaining their legitimacy. In large part, monarchical government derived its authority from its role as the defender and supporter of Shi'ite Islam. Since most of the population shares in the theological belief system of Shi'ism, religion has always been an essential motivational factor for Iranian politicians, from shahs to provincial governors. Popular political support has been accorded the individual who professes religiosity and who faithfully supports Shi'ism; attacks upon Shi'ite Islam are eschewed by astute politicians. The power behind the religious attitude in Iran has been an influential force tapped by wise leaders. When they appeared in the guise of religion, social movements often gained the support of groups that were generally apolitical: for example, the tobacco protest of the nineteenth century, leading to the Constitutional Revolution.[33]

Generally, the ulama considered all secular government imperfect. This belief was based on the theory of the Imamate and has been reflected in their actions, as one writer explains:

> The perfect government is that of the Imam. In his absence every form of government is of necessity imperfect, for the imperfection of men is reflected in their political institutions. The distrust of all worldly government after the disappearance of the Mahdi and the early experiences of the Shi'a community made Twelve-Imam Shi'ism apathetic toward political life until the establishment of the Persian Shi'a Safavid dynasty. During the Constitutional Revolution in Iran from 1905 to 1911 the ulama were again extremely active in agitating for political reform.[34]

Analysis of a few pivotal periods will show how the religious establishment responded to situations that did not accord with Shi'ite Islamic ideas of legitimacy.

Clerical Role and Influence during the Constitutional Era

Representative government, new to Iran in 1906, could not be described as a secular system. Article 1 of the Supplementary Fundamental Laws of the Iranian Constitution of 1907 declared Ithna Ashari Shi'ism the official state religion. Article 2 stated that the National Assembly was founded with the aid of the Twelfth Imam and that laws passed by this body must never be contrary to the sacred precepts of Islam and the laws set forth by the Prophet. Article 39 required the Shah, before acceding to the throne, to take an oath on the Quran promising to preserve the independence of Iran and to propagate the faith. Article 58 required that ministers of the government be Muslims of Iranian descent and nationality. The constitution established a board of five mujtahids empowered to review Majlis laws to assure their congruity with Islamic law. These constitutional provisions demonstrated the influence of clericalism in the Constitutional Revolution of 1905–9. With the disappearance of the Mahdi, the possibility of legitimate exercise of power was lost forever. This thinking had effects on the attitudes and actions of the ulama toward government, particularly during the constitutional period and thereafter, as described by one writer:

> Hence all states are inalienably usurpatory, even those of formal Shi'i affiliation. This usurpatory nature of the state . . . emerged with great clarity in the Qajar period, inspiring a pervasive attitude of repugnance to the state and its representatives. The curbing and limitation of this illegitimate organ, implied in the constitutional concept, were therefore attractive to ulama nurtured in a traditional perspective of distrust of temporal power.[35]

The religious establishment, during the constitutional era, was actively opposed to the onerous conditions of the state brought about by monarchical profligacy and tyranny. The Iranian Constitutional Movement cannot be described as totally secular. This is in contrast to other national movements, such as the French Revolution, in which the church suffered gravely because of its identification with the status quo. Whereas the national movement in France was thoroughly secular, the nationalism of Iran contained elements of both secularism and clericalism. The laity and clergy were united in their opposition to foreign encroachment and monarchical corruption.

An interesting observation made by Norman Jacobs in 1966 concerning the actions of the ulama when they opposed the status quo was certainly true during the constitutional era, but not in 1979: "the clergy when it goes into opposition to the existing order, does not attack *rationally*, nor does it seek to institutionalize its power as a countervailing element in the political realm (political authority), as did the medieval western Christian clergy."[36] Especially important was the ulama's apparent lack of interest in establishing a permanent political power base to continuously carry out their ends. Also, the ulama did not act independently regarding vital issues that affected the society greatly, neither did they seek political power for its own sake or based on a religious theory of political legitimacy. Once immediate goals were realized during the constitutional epoch—the formation of a legislative assembly and tighter controls over the Shah's foreign policy prerogatives—direct political activity by religious leaders subsided.

Sayyed Jamal al-Din "al-Afghani" (1839–97) was one architect in the alliance between religious and secular elements. International traveler and pan-Islamist, Afghani spoke of the need to unite the religious and nonreligious opposition to foreign intrusion. His vociferous attacks against the government attracted a following of clerical intellectuals to his cause. In a letter to Nasir al-Din Shah, Afghani rebuked the Shah's minister for "selling the realms of Islam and the abodes of Mohammed and his household to foreigners."[37] His voice gave inspiration to the Revolution of 1905–9.

The alliance between religious and secular elements of society was influential in the Shah's granting of the Constitution in 1906. In the Constitutional Movement, the ulama demonstrated their ability to act as an effective pressure group. Their association with the popular constitutional cause evinced their independence from the political system. The ulama were effective in initiating social protests and social unity, largely through their communications system and psychological ties with the Iranian people.

When Muzaffar al-Din Shah failed to live up to his earlier promise to consider the question of reforms, and acts of violence against the innocent continued in Tehran and the provinces, a large number of the ulama left Tehran to take bast in Qum in July 1906. This exodus brought a halt to all legal transactions in Tehran. Faced with the termination of judicial action, as well as a general strike in Tehran, the Shah dismissed Ain al-Daula, his vice-regent, and agreed to the establishment of a representative assembly.[38] The coalition of religious leaders, merchants, and intellectuals had been a success in 1906. The religious nature of the confrontation guaranteed the ulama a leadership role, and the ulama were one of the six groups from which delegates to the new National Assembly were chosen.

During the Constitutional Revolution and other national movements that followed, one of the basic motivations of the ulama was their enmity toward foreign (meaning non-Islamic) intrusion into the affairs of Iran. On the issue of national independence, the religious leaders were unyielding. But unlike the other members of the nationalist coalition, the ulama had one other aim—a return to closer adherence to the Quran as a societal model. Given that nationalism requires identification of an individual with the whole community, and that approximately 90 percent of the population of Iran is Shiʿite, it is easy to understand the religious community's significant involvement in preserving national independence from foreign penetration since national and religious independence seemed congruent. The ulama's important part in the Constitutional Revolution is best summed up by the remarks of one observer: "It is generally held, and rightly so, that the most influential force behind the Persian Revolution was the ʿulama's support of the constitutionalists. Had the ʿulama not sanctioned the Revolution, it would definitely have died still born."[39]

The secular repercussions of the Constitutional Movement were issues that religious leaders elected to the Majlis consistently had to face in the postrevolutionary period; they persistently opposed reform measures they believed would increase secular authority.

Postconstitutional Period and Religious Authority

As prime minister, it was popularly expected that Reza Khan would pursue a republican form of government following the example of Turkey. The Shah's initiatives toward republicanism in Iran met with vehement clerical opposition. The protestations of the ulama stemmed from their fear that the severe blow dealt the Muslim clergy in Turkey by secular reforms and the abolition of the caliphate in 1924 would also take place in Iran. Reza Shah attempted to quell clerical agitation by recommending, after talks with religious leaders at Qum, cessation of any future discussion of republican government. Again, the religious leaders had demonstrated their efficacy and strength as a united group.

While overtly displaying religious devotion, Reza Shah set out to dissipate the influence of the ulama. The Shah's dictatorial rule, beginning in 1926, was such as to cause the ulama to regret their earlier decision against republicanism. The political framework of prewar Iran was continued under Reza Shah, but the power of the religious leaders came under attack.

The Shah could not attack Shiʿism directly without jeopardizing his monarchical security; instead he sought to erode clerical power by attacking its strongholds of power: monopolies on education, law, and administrative control of waqf. In 1928, a civil code taken mainly from French sources was adopted. Although matters of personal status were still governed by the Shariʿa, a secular code for marriage and divorce adopted in 1931 further limited the scope of religious law. A secular commercial code was initiated in 1932, and a secular definition of penal crimes in 1936.[40] The Shah attempted to destroy religious influence in state affairs, but he abdicated before his plans came to fruition.

Although Reza Shah had driven many religious leaders into exile or silence, the ulama again gained power after 1941 in the liberal environment that prevailed with the Shah's abdication. The religious establishment was a galvanizing force in the agitations that led to Mossadegh's rise to power and the eventual expulsion of the Anglo-Iranian Oil Company in 1951. During the controversy over nationalization of Iranian oil in the 1950s, the Shi'ite ulama generally supported nationalization and were demonstrative in their opposition to foreign interests.

The xenophobia of Mossadegh's program was an issue that all elements of Iranian society could rally around, especially the ulama, who supported his crusade against an imperialist, non-Muslim power. Along with the issue of national independence, Mossadegh appealed to the ulama because of his recognition of the negative influence upon Iranian society of foreign penetration and his concern with maintaining Iran's distinct cultural heritage. Traditions of the past were not essentially regarded as something to overcome but as a source of inspiration for the present, since it was the imported foreign ideas, not traditional religious values, that were seen as the major cause of Iran's problems.[41]

The support provided the National Front by the religious order was of consequence to the party's efficacy, since certain religious leaders were influential in mobilizing support among segments of the population otherwise apolitical (particularly the lower and lower middle classes). One of the most noted religious leaders, esteemed by the masses and famed for his ability to mobilize a crowd at a moment's notice, was Abol-Qasem Kashani. Kashani played a large role in the political machinations of the 1950s. At least seven other prominent religious leaders, following the lead of the outspoken Kashani, declared it the religious duty of Iranian Muslims to support the Nationalist Movement, with a religious ruling to this effect published by one of the leading mujtahids of the time, Ayatollah Khonsari. Kashani, like Mossadegh, had a great deal of influence with the people.[42] He and his followers were generally regarded as extreme nationalists, but Kashani's control over the Majlis delegation of religious leaders made him a political force to be reckoned with by Mossadegh and the liberal nationalist lay element. The alliance of Mossadegh and Kashani was based on a realization of Kashani's popularity and influence with the masses and on their mutual goal of extirpating the common enemy.

Although a split between Mossadegh and Kashani in 1953 weakened the National Front, many religious leaders remained loyal to Mossadegh and supported the party until his fall from power. The fact that Kashani shifted his support to the royalists was instrumental in Mossadegh's eventual overthrow in 1953. The combined forces of Kashani, the mass support provided by Ayatollah Behbehani, who controlled a large religious-political organization in southern Tehran, and foreign (CIA) intrigue ultimately brought Mossadegh's downfall and reinstated the monarchical rule of the Pahlavis.

One particular religious association, the Fedayan-i Islam (Crusaders for Islam), religious absolutists, were an obtrusive pressure group, whose violent actions had a powerful effect on events in the 1950s. The machinations of the Fedayan, which employed violence as a political weapon, played an important part in the movement to nationalize the AIOC, but they also brought the religious order into disrepute during this period. Although advocating nationalization, the Fedayan's goal was a return to the caliphate, in which the secular and sectarian would blend together. In 1951, a member of the Fedayan killed Prime Minister Ali Razmara, upon whom the West had staked its hopes for a solution to the problem of oil nationalization. The Fedayan was also responsible for an unsuccessful assassination attempt against the Shah in 1949. Even Mossadegh raised their ire by bolstering the secular arm of government. A year after Razmara's death, a Fedayan gunman wounded Foreign Minister Dr. Hossein Fatemi, apparently missing his target, Mossadegh.

The prestige and popularity of the ulama were such as to facilitate their ability to function within the reinstated regime of Shah Mohammad Reza Pahlavi. In addition, Kashani's split with Mossadegh and his support of the royalists were factors abetting this transition. With the new regime, the ulama demonstrated their ability to maneuver within the existing political frame of reference. Under Mohammad Reza Pahlavi's regime, overt respect for the religious order was obligatory, but the ulama's ability to influence events was undermined during this period. The political weapon of popular demonstration was replaced by covert opposition and intrigue.

The Post-Mossadegh Period

The precarious position of Mohammad Reza Pahlavi, as he reassumed political control after Mossadegh's deposition, was a factor in his decision to seek support from the religious leaders. He accepted cooperation from anyone who offered it, favoring ulama with jobs, legislative seats, and religious appointments. The new Shah was well aware of his need for traditional support while still threatened by Nationalist

Front and Communist forces, and he was also cognizant of the legitimacy provided by his association with religion. He promulgated his image as a religious man and described visions in which he saw certain religious leaders such as Ali. These visions were adduced to prove the monarch's continuing spiritual link to the divine force of Islam and the Imamate.

To strengthen his position, the Shah attempted to cultivate an Islamic exterior and to keep the lines of communication with the religious leaders open. He made efforts to keep in touch with Ayatollah Borujerdi, the acknowledged leader of Iranian Shi'ites of the time. This dialogue ceased in 1960 when the government introduced a limited land reform program opposed by Borujerdi on the grounds that it was against Islamic law regarding the rights of private property. Also, the Shah made publicized visits to shrines within Iran and sought the patronage of certain ulama such as Ayatollah Behbehani and Dr. Hossein Imami, who did not shun association with the state. But the Shah's initiatives toward economic development, as a means of weakening the influence of traditionalism and depoliticizing religious institutions, were disconcerting to the clergy, one of the groups most affected by his modernization policies and rigid control. The Shah's awareness of the need to give his rule legitimacy in religious terms while pursuing a policy of modernization, which was often contrary to traditional religious doctrine, produced an ambivalent governmental policy toward the religious establishment, at times repressive and at other times relaxed.

During the postwar period and even after his dubious triumph in 1953, the Shah faced serious opposition and failed to amass the concentrated support necessary for modernization. The process of consolidating his power began with the overthrow of Mossadegh and continued with the violent suppression of dissent in 1963. With the National Front, the Tudeh, and other opposition groups sufficiently contained, the Shah felt secure enough to move on social and economic reforms.[43]

The Ulama and Politics: 1963–79

Between 1954 and 1961, the Shah undertook a concerted program to solidify his position. In his moves toward consolidation, he used coercive political tactics, not unlike those of his father in the 1930s. The Shah set up an extensive security network, strengthening the army and gendarmerie and organizing a secret police system in 1957. His twin programs of reform and coercion were challenged by Iran's religious leaders.

The last decade witnessed a resurgence of the ulama as the leaders of popular opposition to the regime. Three Iranian mujtahids emerged as the spiritual and political leaders of the Shi'ite community in Iran during this period: Ayatollah Mohammad Hadi Milani, resident of Mashad and Azerbaijan; Ayatollah Kazim Shari'atmadari of Qum; and Ayatollah Ruhollah Khumayni, exiled in Najaf, Iraq. Ayatollah Shari'atmadari, a revered Islamic scholar, was one of the most powerful figures inside Iran. An opponent of violence, Shari'atmadari strongly opposed the Shah on constitutional and religious grounds. With Ayatollah Khumayni's outspoken opposition to the Shah and his government, which heightened in 1963, his fame and popularity spread within Iran. He was willing to confront the Shah's regime when few dared to do so. The example Ayatollah Khumayni set in 1963 and his writings and denunciations of the government thereafter established him as a national leader and spokesman for popular aspirations.[44]

The Shah took steps to stabilize his regime and to gain dominance over groups with power in Iranian society, including the religious order. Among his initiatives was the unfolding of his White Revolution in 1963, aimed at domestic politics, emphasizing land reform, electoral reform, economic development, and literacy. The Shah's attempts at government control through his incipient programs were reflected in various moves to establish government-maintained religious schools— superfluous in a country with the long religious tradition of Iran. Governmental intentions seemed clear—to reduce the disruptive influence of Iran's religious leaders by incorporating them into a secularly motivated government.

Although the land reform element of the White Revolution met with opposition from the ulama, in that it encompassed religiously endowed lands, an important source of revenue, this was not the only basis for ulama contention. It appears that one of the main thrusts of religious opposition and criticism of the regime in 1963 was not against reform, but against government autocracy and subservience to Western powers; as Hamid Algar points out, objection appeared to center upon "autocratic rule and violation of the constitution; the proposal to grant capitulatory rights to American advisors and military personnel in Iran and their dependents; the contracting of a $200 million loan from the United States for the purchase of military equipment; and the maintenance of diplomatic, commercial, and other relations with Israel, a state hostile to the Muslims and Islam."[45] The opposition of the ulama to the

Shah and his policies appeared to be based in part on the effects the reforms would have on sustaining the Shah's autocratic rule through controlled elections and centralized control of Iranian society.

Ayatollah Khumayni denounced the White Revolution, preaching against the Shah's rule from his pulpit at the Faiziyeh Madrasa in Qum. On 22 March 1963, the Shah responded by sending paratroopers and the security police to attack the madrasa. A number of students were beaten and killed, and the madrasa was ransacked. Khumayni's denunciations did not stop; confrontation reached its peak in June with the beginning of Muharram, the month when the martyrdom of Imam Hossein is commemorated.[46] The resultant disturbances of 1963 were "the culmination of a movement of resistance to the exercise of arbitrary power by the government, which by the summer of 1963 was felt by some to be intolerable. Fundamentally the movement was a protest by the religious classes against what they believed, rightly or wrongly, to be injustice (zulm)."[47]

Disturbances in Mashad and Qum brought events to a climax. No longer able to tolerate the vociferous denunciations of Ayatollah Khumayni, the Shah had him arrested on 5 June 1963. Unfortunately for the government, the timing of Khumayni's arrest coincided with Muharram. When news of his arrest reached the tazia procession in Tehran, the procession ultimately turned into antigovernment demonstrations. The University of Tehran became the scene of political demonstrations and clashes. Clerical opposition was supported by the Tehran masses; but riots were brutally suppressed by the government, with many religious leaders arrested or exiled. Outbreaks of protest were reported throughout Iran. As the uprising continued in Tehran, tanks and troops surrounded mosques in the capital. A call went out in a Tehran pamphlet for jihad (holy war) against the Shah's regime. Orders had been given the police, army, and security forces to shoot to kill.[48] Six days later the disturbances were finally repressed, but only after armed assaults on the demonstrators by government forces, resulting in the loss of many lives.

Ayatollah Khumayni was released in April 1964, but he continued his defiant and unaccommodating stance against the Shah's regime; his following grew among the middle ranks of the ulama and younger clerics. Khumayni was arrested again in November 1964; this time he was exiled to Turkey. He was granted permission to move to Najaf, Iraq, in 1965. Pilgrims from Iran journeying to Iraq to visit shrines provided a link with Iran. Khumayni led the opposition to the Shah from Najaf. The demonstrations of 1963 in Tehran were historically significant because of the rapprochement between the students in the Nationalist Movement on the campuses and the anti-Shah clergy; this reunion had importance for future revolutionary events in Iran.

The events of 1963 were given special attention in this section to point out the striking role of the ulama during this time, especially that of Ayatollah Khumayni, whose arrest sparked immediate disturbances against the government in Tehran as well as in the provinces. The ulama-led demonstrations, in which many were arrested, evinced their activist role in the political system. Iran's mosques were not only places of learning and prayer but also increasingly became centers for political action. As one dissident lawyer remarked regarding the significance of the religious order in Iran during this epoch: "We have not been allowed to form political parties. We have no newspapers of our own. But the religious leaders have a built-in communications system. They easily reach the masses through their weekly sermons in the mosques and their network of mullahs throughout the nation. That is why so many non-religious elements cloak their opposition in the mantle of religion."[49]

Manifestations of discontent and opposition in Iran continued throughout the 1970s. The antigovernment demonstrations that took place throughout Iran in 1978 and 1979 were largely inspired and led by the religious leaders from the mosques of Iran's cities. Martial law was decreed in Tehran in September 1978, after antigovernment demonstrators and soldiers clashed and many demonstrators were killed. Although the decree declared that gatherings of three or more persons were forbidden, attendance at Friday mosque services was not included. This exclusion demonstrated the government's tenuous position vis-à-vis the Iranian religious order.

The themes of the Constitutional Movement—disdain for autocratic rule and for subservience to foreign powers—ran through the religious opposition to government under Mohammad Reza Pahlavi. As one writer observes:

> There exists, then, a remarkable continuity in the political role of the ulama in Iran, a tradition of opposition to autocratic power that links the nineteenth century with the present. . . . Despite all the inroads of the modern age, the Iranian national consciousness still remains wedded to Shiʿi Islam, and when the integrity of the nation is held to be threatened by internal autocracy and foreign hegemony, protests in religious terms will

continue to be voiced, and the appeals of men such as Āyatullah Khumaynī to be widely heeded.[50]

Beginning with Reza Shah, the political authority exerted greater control over the religious order, but, as we have seen, this did not significantly handicap the ulama. As functionaries providing divine guidance and leadership to the Iranian Shiʿite community in the absence of the Imam, the mujtahids had an inviolable prerogative to oppose secular authority. Commenting upon the mujtahids' participation in antigovernment demonstrations in Qum and Tabriz (1978), a Western observer notes: "They almost certainly had a role in events in Qum—and probably did indirectly in Tabriz. But in both cases, the opposition of which they were a part went beyond their immediate and rather simple but zealous flocks to include middle-class merchants of the Bazaar as well as intellectuals from university campuses and writers' groups."[51]

The ulama were troublesome to the political authority because of their standing and role in the Shiʿite community and their ability to organize and inspire the polity when needed. Shiʿite Islam is a powerful force in Iranian society, and the political authority has always operated in this context. So far we have attempted to examine the relationship between "church" and state in Iran prior to the Islamic Revolution of 1978–79. In the next section we turn to analysis of how Iranians have dealt with political realities through a religious experience.

SHIʿITE WORLD VIEW, EXPRESSION, AND THE POLITICAL SYSTEM

To change means, among other things, to go counter to tradition. Iran is a society rooted in both royal and religious traditions. In a nonparticipatory political system, isolation and retreat, rather than positive social action, were the mechanisms developed by Iranians over the ages as the most feasible means of dealing with the oppressive social-political milieu. In the authoritarian and arbitrary monarchical system of Iran, individuals had little, if any, control and no certain mastery of their future. Iranians in the past generally acted by compromising with the empirical world through inactivity and passive indifference. Only in a few instances, prior to the Islamic Revolution, did the Iranian people challenge this imperious system.

Basic to the Shiʿite world view are the ideas of the evil of injustice, the usurpation of leadership, and the imperfection of temporal existence, all of which can only be rectified by the reappearance and rule of the Hidden Imam. In such a precarious social-political milieu, Iranians were preconditioned to perceive the negative, the sad, and the tragic. Hope for change, for the restoration of righteousness and justice, is expressed in Iranian Shi'ism through the return of the Imam Mahdi. Islamic history is seen as a gradual decline from a pristine past, beginning with the golden age of the Prophet. In an environment of injustice and evil, Iranians sought alleviation through their religious history, which was mythologized. One of Iran's most symbolic religious figures is Imam Hossein, who is very much alive in the Iranian spirit. His stand against the forces of evil and injustice, sacrificing himself for the temporal and eternal safety of his people, led to the growth of an intimate association between Hossein's act and the political process in Iran.

Political Expression and Muharram

Clyde Kluckhohn writes that ritual is "often a symbolic dramatization of the fundamental 'needs' of the society, whether 'economic,' 'biological,' 'social,' or 'sexual.' Mythology is the rationalization of these same needs, whether they are all expressed in overt ceremonial or not. . . . Ceremonials tend to portray a symbolic resolvement of the conflicts which external environment, historical experience, and selective distribution of personality types have caused to be characteristic in the society."[52] As we shall see, the expression of social needs and conflict resolution that sprang from the oppressive conditions of Iranian social-political processes have been portrayed through religious ritual and ceremonies.

One of the politically most significant of these ceremonies takes place during the month of Muharram. The first month of the Islamic lunar year marks the beginning of an annual month of mourning for Imam Hossein, who, according to Shi'ite tradition, was killed by Caliph Yazid, his rival, while on his way to receive the caliphate. Hossein and loyal followers were slain by Yazid's soldiers at Karbala circa A.D. 680. The event of Hossein's martyrdom is commemorated during this month at *rozeh'khani* gatherings, usually presided over by mullahs. These ceremonies reach their peak on the tenth day of the month in the tazia, in which the tragic death of Hossein is reenacted. The public ceremonies surrounding the tazia are characterized by effusive displays of unrestrained mourning and self-flagellation, in which large crowds gather and parade through the streets.[53]

Although the focus of Muharram is on the martyrdom of Hossein, the implications are broader. The conflict between Hossein and Yazid was principally a political event because it was concerned with the question of "who should make and carry out decisions regarding public policy and the common good."[54] There were political implications for contemporary Iranian politics in the events at Karbala and the symbol of Hossein. This conflict was seen as a symbolic struggle between Hossein, who represented purity, goodness, and the spiritual, and Yazid, who represented evil and the debauchery of temporal existence. The reenactment of the drama is for Shi'ites both a protest against injustice and a celebration of the victory of good over evil. In times of social change in Iran, Hossein has been the symbol of national unity. Confrontation and expression were suppressed in the monarchical political system. Therefore, the drama of Hossein was a vehicle for the expression of social conditions and attitudes. "Because of the feeling of the insufficiency of ordinary action, mythic and ritual enactments of the drama of Husayn are utilized to express and activate their feelings while selected meanings are singled out for emphasis."[55]

Through these ceremonies, the Iranian people vicariously released social and political feelings, long suppressed. The costumes worn in the drama revealed social conflicts or long-held animosities; for example, after the annexation of several Iranian provinces by the tsars, the Russians (represented through costumes) appeared in the tazia as the evil-doers. Commenting upon the ceremonies in relation to the authoritarian regime of the late Shah, one observer in 1961 suggested: "Many participants are said to mentally transfer the sufferings and injustices which accompanied Husain's martyrdom to their current personal and national sufferings and injustices. While mourning over the social and political evils which killed Husain, they are at the same time mourning over current social and political evils and are perhaps also publicly expressing sorrow for their personal contribution to them."[56] Like Hossein, Shi'ite Muslims in the power of Iran's monarchs knew what it was to suffer under unjust and venal rule. Imam Hossein, it is believed, chose to die rather than abjure what he regarded as his right to the caliphate. As a martyr for justice, and as an example of righteous suffering, Hossein is seen as the paradigm and inspiration for the return of the Mahdi. Imam Hossein's importance to the Iranian people as a religious and political redeemer and innovator is captured in an excerpt from a sermon given by Sayyed Mahmud Taleghani during the month of Muharram in 1963, shortly before the riots and demonstrations against the government. Taleghani quoted from one of Imam Hossein's speeches:

> People, God's Prophet has said that if there is an oppressive sultan breaking God's promises, committing sin among the people, disregarding God's orders and acting against God's messenger, it is the duty of everyone who is aware of these to stand against him to try to change him either with advice, or if this is not possible, with power. If one keeps quiet, then God will give him the same punishment as he gives to the sultan. Because by being quiet, he has acted as his partner in crime.[57]

Although expressed in religious vernacular, Imam Hossein's message is revolutionary. The persistence of ritual surrounding the martyrdom of Hossein results from its satisfaction of fundamental social-political needs of the Iranian people. The tyranny in contemporary Iran as in the past gave life to an ancient event. The revolutionary symbol of Hossein was used frequently during and after the Islamic Revolution of 1978–79. Shi'ite symbols were used as revolutionary images and Shi'ite martyrs as revolutionary heroes and models for political activism during the Islamic Revolution. Religious history and symbols, pervasive in Iranian society, have been a traditional force to galvanize the polity against perceived political injustice.

The people's strong desire for a deliverer is implicit in the Iranians' devotion to Imam Hossein. The tacit feelings of despair over a lost history and hope for deliverance evidenced during Muharram were channeled and contained within the limits of religious expression. These feelings, when expressed outside the confines of religion, would prove to be a potent revolutionary force. The month-long engagement with the themes of Muharram, which are externally religious but reveal underlying political dimensions, stimulated a certain solidarity within the Iranian community, providing a set of common understandings.

The power of Muharram to draw large numbers of people to a public expression of latent political discontent, the reevaluation of self and society, and hope in a "savior" suggested a deep societal restiveness and strong nationalistic force finding expression through religion. The cohesive force of religion in Iranian society is visibly demonstrated during this special period, and at all times through the symbol of Imam Hossein.

We seek answers to the existential question of the human situation in various ways; for Iranians, religion provided a form of security in an insecure political system. During periods of political upheaval in Iran, religion galvanized the support of what might generally be regarded as society's submissive groups. Religion was an untapped source of political power.

SUMMARY

In Iranian society, culture, religion, and ethnic ties have been stronger than the political bond. No political entity has been able to supplant religion as a source of national identity. As early as 1959, one observer noted that "the sacred law of Islam is inwardly felt and is often more binding than the law of the state."[58] The association of Shi'ite Islam with Iranian national identity contributed to its staying power, despite growing secularization of the society under the late Shah. Although the experience and practice of being a Shi'ite Muslim has undergone transformation in modern Iran, profession of that faith is still an important part of being Iranian.

In a country replete with distrust, especially of those in authority, the people have had a basic trust and faith in their religious leaders. A good deal of confidence and power has been given to the religious order, based in part on the Shi'ite belief that the mujtahids provide guidance in matters of practice in the absence of the Mahdi. Trust in religious leaders is exemplified by the prominence and following of Ayatollah Khumayni. He was esteemed even though he was expelled from the country; when he was in Paris (1978) his message was still received and followed. Iran's history evinces the conflict between political and religious authority based on the trusteeship of the mujtahids. A mujtahid, in order to maintain his following, must be *pak* (clean), literally uncorrupted. The mujtahids' relationship with their followers made them the conduits for protest in the past.

In a country where group activity and cooperative interpersonal relations have been the exception rather than the rule, religious leaders demonstrated their ability to organize the people in pursuit of a special yet common interest. While Iranians generally tended to find it more efficient to pursue their aims individually through personal contacts and other affiliations, their political interests have been articulated through the group pressure of the religious order—for example, in the Constitutional Revolution, oil nationalization, the protests of 1968 and 1978, and the new form of government. The mosque has been the center of religious, social, and political activity and has historically provided bast in times of political dissent. In the cities the larger mosques are nearly always located in the bazaars, historically the center of political communication and activism.

The interplay of political and religious authority is an interesting phenomenon in the political culture of Iran. As one writer points out, "The traditional character of Iranian society still defines the boundaries within which the process of modernization must operate."[59] The fact that most of the population shares in the theological belief system of Ithna Ashari Shiʿism represents a vital national force in contemporary Iran. As we have seen, the political authority historically found it difficult to challenge the religious order without jeopardizing its legitimacy with the people. In the past, the monarchs were acutely aware of this fact as they formulated programs and policies. The paradox of monarchical authority revolved around its desire to attenuate the power of the religious order, while concomitantly desiring religious legitimacy, to assure for itself the loyalty of the masses.

To move Iran from its traditionalism, the Pahlavi regime pursued a policy of rapid economic development; implicit in such a policy was the secularization of society. According to Shiʿism, and as stipulated in the Supplementary Fundamental Laws of 1907, the government (the Shah) was to protect and defend the Shiʿite faith. Therefore, in the eyes of the religious authority, the government was not fulfilling its temporal role as guardian of the Shiʿite community in the absence of Imam Mahdi. In terms of governmental output, the religious authority expected the political authority to seek a return to the orthodox principles of Shiʿism and to make governmental decisions congruent with Shiʿite Islamic doctrine, not to usurp the power of the ulama.

Although many of the urban reform-minded in Iranian society turned away from the orthodoxy of Islam, the influence and power of the religious authority was a vital factor in the decisions made by the Pahlavi regime. It was a commentary on the late Shah's government that, with its unlimited physical power and control, it dared not abandon its religious connection, cognizant of the support derived from it.

Religion has been and continues to be a powerful force in the sociopolitical system of Iran. Prior to 1979, members of the clergy were viewed as moral and political critics and guides to society; their participation in daily politics was ambiguous. With the Islamic Revolution, direct involvement of members of the clergy in politics will inevitably alter their moral and political authority, possibly resulting in a diminution of both.

Throughout this chapter, we have examined the pervasive role of Shi'ite Islam and religious leaders in the social-political life of Iran. For centuries the daily lives of Iranians have been guided by the Shi'ite religious order, whose influence encompassed not only the spiritual life of the country, but its secular and economic institutions as well. It is not surprising, then, that in times of internal strife and frustration Iranians looked to their religious leaders for succor and leadership. Nowhere in the Middle East do the ulama wield as much political power and authority as in Iran. Their ability to unite the people for political action has been of paramount importance. The political power of the religious order is markedly visible from the period of the Constitutional Revolution to the present. The religious-nationalist alliance forged during the Constitutional Revolution, revived during the 1950s over the issue of oil nationalization and during other periods of strife, was a formidable threat to the Pahlavi dynasty, inevitably leading to the demise of the monarchical system, the subject of the concluding chapter of this book. A fear that loomed large for the regime was complete alienation from the religious community, thereby losing a base of legitimacy. This check of the people on government was vital in a country ruled by an absolute monarch, where inputs into the political process did not exist. In the authoritarian political milieu of the past, religion was necessary as a control mechanism over the power of the state.

Religion is a deep-rooted cultural norm in Iran; and as discussed in the last chapter, the voice of the ulama in the Islamic government is more stentorian today than it has ever been. The message of the ruling ulama is for a return to orthodoxy. The authoritarianism, elitism, and hierarchy of of Shi'ism find expression in the Islamic government of Iran, headed by a Vali-ye-faqih, the supreme political guide. The Islamic Revolution produced an authoritarian government with some elements seen in the past; the milieu has changed from secularism to clericalism. The monarch as the head of state has been replaced by the Vali-ye-faqih, Ayatollah Khumayni, who holds ultimate political authority. Other government positions are delegated to a religious elite, rather than a secular elite. The Islamic government follows the theocratic political heritage of Shi'ism, in which sovereignty resided in the Imams and ulama, not in the people. In a country long accustomed to authoritarian rule in religion and politics, constitutional government has had no precedent. Politics in the Islamic Republic of Iran accommodates a displayed trust in the masses. The ruling ulama use the messianic language and metaphors of Shiʿism to maintain influence and power. It is a politics of confrontation against the rich and intellectuals, and attacks the perceived injustice exercised by large nations against the less developed.

As noted at the beginning of this chapter, Islam embraces all aspects of life, not merely the metaphysical and spiritual. Consequently, in terms of Islamic tradition, the blending of the religious and secular/ political in Shiʿite Iran is a natural phenomenon. The union of religious and secular forces during pivotal periods in Iranian history merely reinforces the holistic approach and foundation of Shiʿite Islam. As we have seen, Shiʿism in Iran appears to encompass an authoritarian tradition, through the norms and ideas of leadership, elitism, and obedience. At the same time, through its checks and challenges to political authority, it has seemingly maintained an antiauthoritarian tradition.

The Shiʿite religious tradition is a powerful symbol in Iranian culture and national identity, and its religious leaders have been important protagonists in the unfolding political drama. This chapter has focused on analyzing the prominent role of religion in shaping the political culture of Iran prior to the Islamic Revolution. The next chapter concentrates on the social beliefs and norms of Iranian society in order to capture the cultural nuances that shape the political system.

IV

Sociological Linkages and Political Culture

Within a particular cultural tradition each individual is inducted into the social system. Cultural values and behaviors that shape a particular society are transmitted directly and indirectly to the individual. When the focus is on becoming a member of society, the term *socialization* applies. This section examines shared values and behaviors that form the sociocultural experience of the Iranian people and establish a link to the political system.

Cultural phenomena that make the social system of Iran distinctive will aid in understanding the structure and performance of the Iranian political system. The legitimacy of the political system, its authority, its decision-making and conflict-resolving processes are based on "the appraisal of action in terms of shared or common values in the context of the involvement of the action in the social system."[1] As one observer remarks: "Because all modern governments need a substantial degree of public support in order to survive and develop politically, the role of culture in furthering or impeding a sense of national identity and loyalty is a matter of great concern to students of developmental politics. The ability of citizens to cooperate greatly affects the capacity of the political system to create viable organizations."[2]

This chapter emphasizes analysis of the cultural variables unique to the socialization process in Iran that affect the maintenance and operation of the political system: the family, education, and the literary-artistic milieu.

In studying the political culture of Iran in the context of socialization, it should be borne in mind that Western penetration fostered among modernists and secularists a reevaluation of "old" values and norms and to some degree transformed, at least on the surface, the socialization agents in Iranian society. Although Iran underwent dramatic change in recent decades, traditional values and norms have persisted. It should also be noted that change in Iran under the Pahlavi regime took place without any participation by the Iranian people. Modernization was imposed from above by the policies of a select elite and by foreign sources. Economic development in Iran was not organic; it had little relationship to the infrastructure of Iranian society. The enforced and sudden modernization of Iranian society, with its unequal distribution of wealth, brought a backlash against and restiveness toward change and created a climate of conservatism and return to the traditional values espoused in Shi'ite Islam.

This chapter begins by examining the structure of the Iranian social system. With this foundation, we shall analyze the salient cultural variables transmitted from generation to generation that, by their very nature, seem to affect the political system in Iran. The cultural variables identified here should create a basis for understanding the political milieu of Iranian society.

SOCIAL STRUCTURE OF IRANIAN SOCIETY

The idea presented in the eleventh century by an Iranian scholar, Nizam al-Mulk, that over every authority God has placed a higher authority describes the sociopolitical structure of Iran.[3] From its early beginnings, Iranian society has known social gradations.

The class divisions maintained throughout Iran's great dynasties, which collapsed with the fall of the Sassanian, were resurrected by the Safavid dynasty (circa 1500–1736) and continued by the Qajars (1796–1925). Essentially, the basic structure of a ruling class, middle class, and lower class existed over the ages, but the composition of the classes changed, based on the nature of leadership and development. For example, during the Qajar period at the apex of power were the rulers (the shahs) and members of their families. The importance of the tribes and the number of tribal khans among the ruling class were based on the military strength they provided the regime. Civil bureaucrats with administrative responsibilities were followed in rank by important religious leaders. Because of economic development in the eighteenth and nineteenth centuries, the merchant class was, for the first time, explicitly defined as a distinct group with greater rank than the mass of peasants and "menials" at the bottom of the social structure.

The political reform movement of the twentieth century did little to change the traditional social structure of Iranian society in terms of the three major classes—the dominant upper class, urban middle class, and the lower class (made up largely of peasants). Although the traditional social structure supported three different social characters—dominant, independent, and submissive—a balance among them was maintained. The traditional middle class of merchants, artisans, and scholars maintained its independence through dealings with all strata of society and through creative endeavors. Also, its autonomy was strengthened through participation in guilds and other informal associations. The lower classes, particularly the rural peasants and urban laboring classes, manipulated within their group. Over time, "This independent element has increasingly succumbed to new social pressures, while the former dominant and submissive groups have kept relatively to their accustomed ways."[4]

The definitive nature of the Iranian social structure always existed, with positions within the social hierarchy well defined and recognized. This recognition of position was evinced in the wide acceptance of standards of interpersonal behavior reflected in the Iranians' elaborate and ritualistic modes of address, deferential behavior to superiors, and other forms of discourse and social conduct.[5] Class distinctions are recognized and speech and manners adjusted in concert with these preconceptions.

Iran has been essentially an "open" society in the sense that it has remained free of a rigid caste system and a hereditary nobility. As James Bill states, "Iranian society has been marked and profoundly influenced by a structure of interrelated classes. . . . This system of class relationships has exhibited a flexibility and resiliency that has enabled it to persist for nearly 1,400 years."[6] There is little doubt that wealth and power have gone hand-in-hand in Iran for centuries, with wealth frequently a requisite for political office. *Madakhel* (perquisite), the practice of selling positions, made offices available to the individuals willing to pay the highest price. Historically this practice facilitated mobility in Iran. Although social mobility was always a possibility in Iran and classes were sometimes bridged, mobility has always been difficult and certainly not common.[7] Iranians of low status lacked not only the wealth but the means to facilitate the acquisition of wealth, such as formal education, military position, marriage, and access to persons of power. Individuals could move from one class to another through guile, ability, or good fortune. The legendary tale of Hajji Baba of Isfahan is a personification of just such an individual, who, fortuitously and through his own devices, crosses class lines with ease.[8] Traditionally, military or religious service offered the most propitious opportunity for social mobility in Iran.

In addition to the idea that mobility was possible, since the only criterion seemed to be the acquisition of wealth rather than some innate attributes of individual superiority, the absence of an aristocracy or nobility made interclass movement more plausible. One's lineage did not appear to be a hindrance to mobility. The absence of nobility in Iranian society stems from a general lack of value related to genealogy. This did not apply to certain members of the religious order who could trace their descent to the Prophet, or various tribal leaders, or Qajars who relished their kingly lineage. The myth of an "open class" system appears to have been one factor that lessened class conflict, so likely to occur in a tightly knit social structure. Regarding class relationships as they have existed in Iran, one observer notes:

> Iran's rather rigidly defined social structure in which mobility was always, nonetheless, a possibility gave a highly "democratic" tinge to the society, "for every man sees a chance of someday profiting by the system of which he may for the moment be the victim and as the present hardship or exaction is not to be compared in ratio with the pecuniary advantage which he may ultimately expect to reap, he is willing to bide his time and to trust to the fall of the dice in the future."[9]

The reality of the Iranian social structure demonstrated that social class and rank, and the privileges commensurate with social gradations, have existed in Iran. For centuries Iran, like other societies in the Middle East, consisted of a broad base of peasants and tribal groups who "constitute the productive masses upon whose steady labor and docile obedience rests the second group, the comparatively small but powerful elite which reigns and rules."[10]

The Upper/Ruling Class

Prior to the Islamic Revolution, the traditional upper class consisted of six major components: the shahs; the family of the reigning dynasty; tribal nobility; native landlords; system-supporting high ulama; and military elite. The monarch maintained his detachment from the rest of the upper class because of the prodigious power of his position. The above-mentioned groups constituted the ruling class of Iran for centuries. But with the influx of British and Russian influence in the early nineteenth century, nascent groups gained a foothold into the traditional upper class; among these were foreign industrialists and businessmen. In addition to foreign interests drawn to Iran because of its oil wealth, an indigenous economic industrial aristocracy and landless rentier elite appeared principally after World War II; this included a large contingent of wealthy merchants, bankers, contractors, financiers, and industrialists.[11] As in the case of foreign industrialists and entrepreneurs, the indigenous industrial aristocracy was closely related to the other upper-class groups, especially to the royal family, which controlled the largest Iranian businesses.

Aristocracy and dominance in Iran were commensurate with the ownership of large amounts of land, which implied power derived from social prestige and political and economic influence. The royal family, tribal leaders, and high ulama were three of the largest native landowning groups in Iran. Traditionally, large landowners sagaciously maintained close contact with the government as a way of preserving and furthering their own interests. Most of the large landowners lived in luxury in the cities, particularly in the capital, close to the seat of power—away from their estates—while their interests were tended by chosen representatives. In 1960, 80 to 85 percent of all cultivable land in Iran was in the hands of a few hundred landowning families.[12] In addition to owning most of the land, this elite group occupied key positions in government, the top bureaucracy, and the judiciary and was influential in the army and police.

Some Iranians made their way into the upper class through study abroad and scholarship and by marriage or other means of social contact. Downward mobility was also possible, brought on by intrigue, jealousy, or political opposition. Reza Shah's program of land confiscation was also a factor in downward mobility. During Reza Shah's reign, wealthy landowners found themselves confronting a monarch who treated them publicly with disrespect, appeared oblivious to their traditional position in society, and seemed bent upon minimizing their position. Opposition to governmental authority by landowners during Reza Shah's rule was based upon the unorthodox methods used to carry out his policies.

Because of the leisure guaranteed by wealth, the upper class generally was the group that preserved the intellectual and artistic tradition of Iran. Paternalism flourished within this class, based primarily upon hierarchical status as owners of land worked by deferential peasants.

Generally, wealth ensured close contact with those personages in positions of power in government. To preserve lucrative interests, the upper class became a system-supporting group. Only when their interests were in jeopardy did members of this class act; for example, during the Constitutional Revolution, the wealthy landowners sided with the constitutionalists generally to protect their interests against the recklessness and profligacy of the Qajar monarchs. From the time of its establishment, large landowners generally dominated the Majlis and occupied prominent positions within the political system. After Reza Shah's abdication, large landowners asserted control over the Majlis and occupied the majority of ministerial posts; during the oil nationalization controversy, most of them threw their support to Mossadegh. Politically members of the upper class generally sided with the individual or group most amenable to their interests at the time.

The Lower Classes

At the other extreme of the social scale were the vast numbers of poor, powerless, and uneducated people, living in rural walled villages throughout Iran. Since Iran is predominantly an agricultural country, the peasants constitute the largest element in the lower class, but this class has also traditionally consisted of sizable numbers of workers and nomads. The lower class can be segregated according to the following groups: (1) working class; (2) peasant proprietors (work their own land); (3) landless peasantry; and (4) tribal masses. In the late 1950s to early 1960s over one-half of Iranians in the working class were employed in construction, manufacturing, and crafts.[13]

There was no marked alteration in the peasants' way of life, even with Mohammad Reza Pahlavi's attempts at land distribution and administration. Peasants who owned their land occupied a higher status than tenant farmers. Submission to authority among the lower classes stemmed from the socioeconomic dependency of the peasants, who relied upon the landlord for food, shelter, medicine, and the like. Peasants were often the victims of other classes. Their life was made more burdensome and precarious because of their subservient position vis-à-vis the landlords, merchants, and government officials, all inclined to extract something. An example of capricious rule that affected the lower classes was an onerous tax imposed by Reza Shah on the sale of tea and sugar to finance the construction of a railroad. These two items were basic to the peasants' diet, and the tax hurt them particularly. The peasants' lack of control over their lives and livelihoods fostered an environment of suspicion and distrust. In such an environment, the peasants' greatest security was found within their own walled village. Interpersonal relations centered on the primary unit, the family, with religion offering another dimension to a seemingly circumscribed and often hostile social milieu.

The disadvantageous position of the lower classes required the development of a certain guile, necessary to the protection of life and improvement of status. Stories abound concerning the native intelligence of the Iranian peasants, as they learned to play one side against the other; for example, the landlord's representative against the landlord himself. The conservative and religious bent of the lower classes, particularly the peasants, contributed in the past to their general support of the monarchical institution. One reason that the Shah granted concessions (land reform) in the 1960s to the peasants was to garner their support in preserving the traditional system, because he faced the ever-increasing dissatisfaction and disquiet from members of the professional middle class.[14] The late Shah's maneuvers to solidify his position are examined in more detail in the following chapter.

Tribespeople

Although the nomadic masses are a component of the lower class, a tribal elite also existed within the ruling class. As one writer observes, "This alternating membership of tribal khans in the ruling class has tended to soften class lines for most tribal groups since their leaders have moved in and out of the ruling class through the years."[15] The Seljuq and Qajar dynasties originated directly from leaders of tribal groups; others, such as the Safavid, came to power with tribal support.

Unlike the peasants, who led a settled life, the nomads, because of their transient life-style, usually had more freedom from government intrusion (such as taxation) and greater leverage in managing their own affairs. The tribes have persistently played a key role in Iranian history and from earliest times have maintained their independence, acknowledging the authority of their khans (leaders) only.[16] The autonomy of the tribes was a constant source of consternation to the political authority, in that they escaped the authority of the central government, which could never be sure of their continued loyalty. Military support for the monarch and recruitment of troops came largely from the tribes, who for centuries made up Iran's main military strength. Generally, tribal khans maintained governance of their own areas. Tribal control over specific areas was evident in the early 1900s with the presence of the British in Iran; the British paid subsidies to local chiefs for the use of land for oil exploration. Negotiations for a refinery at Abadan in 1909 were conducted with the sheikh of Mohammerah, who was to receive a share of the oil profits. Security at the site was entrusted to local chiefs.[17]

To maintain security and control over the country, Reza Shah's policy was to contain the tribes, which he saw as a threat to his regime; this policy was largely successful, due to his creation of a strong central army. Disarmament, conscription into the armed services, resettlement/settlement of tribal groups, and execution of some of the leading tribal khans were some of the methods used to weaken tribal influence in the country.

The Middle Class

The middle class in Iran is the most heterogeneous of the classes and has been a sociopolitical force throughout Iran's history. It has experienced a great deal of change over the years. Traditionally, the middle class was largely composed of entrepreneurial groups such as bazaar merchants, artisans, the ulama, and members of the bureaucracy. The ulama controlled and benefited from the traditional educational system of maktabs and madrasahs, which emphasized religion and rote learning.

During the twentieth century, this class expanded rapidly with growing numbers of government bureaucrats, office workers, and intellectuals, who frequently were the children of the traditional merchants and artisans. The middle class or "professional bureaucratic intelligentsia" was defined as a group whose power stemmed from skill and talent rather than ownership; its members were basically nonentrepreneurial and obtained a modern higher education. Intellectuals were an important group in this class, but it also included technocrats, administrators, managers, clerks, and the like.[18] Ironically, this new element within the traditional middle class, which was to prove a thorn in the side of the political authority, was the indirect creation of Reza Shah's modernization policies and educational reforms and Mohammad Reza Pahlavi's own development policies. Opposition to the Shah was the strongest among members of the middle class: bureaucrats, bourgeoisie, and ulama. When their interests and those of the nation were threatened, they worked in harmony to achieve desired goals. This was evidenced during the Constitutional Revolution, when the thrust for change emanated from the traditional middle class, especially the bourgeoisie and ulama, who felt most vulnerable to capricious governmental policies of the day. Also, support for oil nationalization and Mossadegh's government was strongest among members of the middle class. Their strength reached its zenith during the Islamic Revolution of 1978–79.

Unlike members of the bureaucratic middle class, who essentially were a part of the governmental apparatus and, therefore, were dependent upon the ruling class and, infrequently, the representatives of the lower class, the bourgeois middle class traditionally maintained a degree of autonomy, with few members moving into the upper class. The intimacy and close proximity of the entrepreneurial class to the bazaar provided the cohesion and organization necessary for sociopolitical action. Throughout Iran's history, the bazaar has been the center of political activity. Many of the framers of Iran's first constitution belonged to conservative clergy and prosperous bazaar groups, whose reforms were largely dictated by self-interests. The importance of the bazaar to the sociopolitical life of Iran was noted by Jamsheed Behnam in 1968:

> The bazar, indeed, does not confine its activities to those of a market, but functions also as a political and social force. . . . In a country where the political parties and syndicates play an insignificant part, this concentration of merchants and trader-craftsmen, living under the shelter of the brick vaults of the bazar in complete unity and solidarity—without being officially organized for the purpose—is an essential element. Apart from the clergy, it is the only force that dares consistently to defy the governing classes and the landed proprietors.[19]

The bazaar has been a unique source of power because of its impact on the economic life of the country and its organization, an element generally lacking in the framework of Iranian society. The merchants and artisans organized into effective guilds and corporations functioning independently of the state. They acted within self-imposed rules of conduct and as a support system in times of need. This solidarity could be used, as it was during the Constitutional Revolution and Islamic Revolution, to put a halt to the economic life of the country by closing the doors of the bazaar in protest, thereby forcing the ruling elite to accede to their demands. The solidarity and power of the bazaar was matched only by that of the ulama, and at times superseded that of the clerical class. The role of the bazaar as the center of political organization and activity was enhanced by its close interrelationship with the ulama, who generally have been the principal agents in opposing oppressive governmental policies. Mosques in the cities are located mainly in the bazaars, and the ulama are an integral part of the life of the bazaar. As the center of communication, economics, and religion, the bazaar has been a dominant force in the sociopolitical life of Iran for centuries.[20] It was central to the flow of information and the creation of public opinion in the absence of a formal, uncontrolled communications system. The importance of the bazaar was particularly evident during the overthrow of Shah Mohammad Reza Pahlavi in 1979; much of the revolutionary communication and planning took place in the bazaar.

In former times the bazaar could effectively restrain the government because it was economically independent, but with Mohammad Reza Pahlavi's efforts at economic centralization and the establishment of banks and Western technology, the bazaar's independence and influence waned. Although not the force it once was, the bazaar continued to play a vital role in the political life of the country.

Unlike the traditional middle class, the new middle class displayed a certain political and economic insecurity. As we shall see in the following chapter, this insecurity was based partially on the dependence of this class on the political apparatus of the late Shah. But as a group it has been a social force with considerable power, stemming from the need for skilled managerial and technical talent to carry out governmental programs and from the sheer weight of its numbers. The Shah was well aware that with such a large number of government employees, government could be brought to a standstill if this group was properly organized.

Economic development, educational opportunities, and contact with the West contributed to the growth of the new middle class and the challenges it presented to the political system. Economic growth in Iran was sudden, unlike the gradual development of Western industrialization. Local conditions did not organically produce this growth; it was introduced externally. Great wealth was traditionally concentrated in the hands of a very few, with poverty the lot of the majority. Although the old economic balance was tipped somewhat, the dissatisfaction of many over the unequal distribution of economic resources remained a constant source of tension among the middle class and other segments of Iranian society.

From the foundation of the Iranian social structure presented thus far, we proceed to a discussion of the cultural norms and values that spring from this social system and how they are linked to the Iranian political system.

SOCIALIZATION AND THE POLITICAL SYSTEM

The socialization process begins when individuals are born into a particular social system. In essence, societal norms and values act upon individuals, who in turn generally act within accepted social patterns. But individuals are also capable of acting upon the social system, thereby effecting change within it. Over time and through the developmental process, individuals are exposed to the influences and patterns of the society in which they live and interact. As members of society they develop cognitive, affective, and evaluative orientations to relate to social objects.

Easton and Dennis, in *Children in the Political System*, state that "socialization consists exclusively of a transmission process whereby orientations and behaviors are passed from one generation to another."[21] Every social system contains a multitude of mechanisms for transmitting its orientations and behaviors, and these mechanisms undoubtedly influence and limit to some degree the personal choices of individuals. But although the inputs of the socialization process may be similar, the way individuals internalize these inputs varies. Socialization need not imply conformity. This is an important concept in terms of cultural change and challenges presented by individuals to an existing social system.[22]

Implicit in the concept of socialization is the idea of induction and acquisition of knowledge, skills, and dispositions that make people functional members of society. If socialization is viewed as a continuous and volatile process rather than a static one, it might be said that, depending upon the elasticity of the social system, people are capable of changing the social system and that resistance to social change is grounded in the conservatism of the initial socialization process.

Socialization is essential in terms of the form and function of a political system, which is an element of the larger social system. The relationship of individuals to the political system is also based on the social norms and values passed on through the socialization process. Orientations to the political system are a determinant of how that system operates and of its continued maintenance or instability and its capacity for political development.

Although Iran is experiencing political and social evolution, the norms and values described in this chapter have been inherent in Iranian society for centuries and continue to affect the sociopolitical process in the country.

In analyzing the social patterns of Iranian society as they relate to the political system, the most pronounced factor in the way that system has functioned over time is the duality of authoritarianism and individualism, or antiauthoritarianism. This duality and the orientations and behaviors manifested because of this phenomenon are analyzed in the following section.

Authoritarianism and Individualism in Iranian Society

Iran is an authoritarian society with what seem to be dominant and submissive behavior patterns learned early in life. The societal demand for submission to authority extends to the leader of the nation, to those who hold a position higher than oneself, and to parents. While Iranian culture displays a certain authoritarian nature, the anomaly lies in the strain of independence that runs through its social fabric. Both acceptance and rejection of authority seem to loom large in Iranian culture. The key element in this paradox appears to be that the demand for submission to authority and its external acceptance has not essentially been accompanied by respect for authority on the part of Iranians. It appears that along with a conscious acceptance of authority is a subliminal rejection of that same authority. This duality is lucidly unfolded in Fereidoun Esfandiary's novel *The Day of Sacrifice*, which revolves around a young man's unceasing internal struggle between two opposing forces; on one hand, obedience to authority; on the other, rejection of that same authority. Authority in this novel is represented by the protagonist's father. The drama revolves around the son's obligation to his father and his continual disregard in fulfilling that obligation, which leads to a tragic yet enlightened conclusion for the son. This piece by Esfandiary points up the strong emotional and physical bond of son to father in Iranian culture. The need for approbation from the father is matched by a rebellion against the onerous burden felt by the son because of the imposing position and overwhelming role of the father. Only when his father's position of authority is shaken does the son see him as a man capable of emotion and despair over the loss of his prized son. Only in his eventual destruction (imprisonment and death), brought on through his own internal struggle and external behavior, does the son resolve the struggle.[23]

In a comparative analysis of Turkey and Iran, Richard N. Frye notes that "Turkish respect for authority is matched by the Persian lack of it. This makes the task of government in Turkey much easier than in Iran. During the reign of Reza Shah, the Persians certainly obeyed the dictator but they did so with the cynicism and Hajji Baba-ness of which only the Persians are capable."[24]

The following Iranian children's story illustrates the feeling that authority was not to be trusted and that government was perceived as being venal: ". . . two boys fall to arguing over who should get a walnut they find. They finally call on a passerby to serve as a judge in the classic Moslem tradition. He gives one half of the shell to one boy, the other half to the other boy, and eats the kernel himself as his wages for deciding the dispute."[25] The lesson of this story is not a moral one for Iranians, since they do not interpret it to mean that the boys should not squabble over the walnut or authority will intercede to teach them a lesson; rather it is interpreted to mean that "if they get involved with authority it will step in and steal from both of them."[26] The arbitrary nature of authority in Iran seems to have led to an underlying need to protect oneself from it. In the social milieu of insecurity and suspicion that was fed by monarchical regimes based on capricious, personal rule and oppression, falsification evolved into a method of protection and a matter of habit.

The Iranian paradox of at once accepting and rejecting authority appears to have developed as a survival mechanism. The socially graded structure of Iranian society figured largely in this atmosphere. The symbol of ultimate power and dominance in Iran was the monarchy, with lesser degrees of power passed to various levels of society, such as viziers, tribal khans, landlords, and village chiefs. At the nadir of all ranks were the peasants and tribespeople, who because of socioeconomic dependency on the dominant groups submitted to all forms of authority. Long centuries of invasion and oppressive rule quickened the Iranian instinct for survival. The uncertainty and impermanence of existence appear to have developed the art of circuity of thought and action in order to retain life and honor. As a means of survival in an authoritarian state, Iranians adopted an intricate code of social relations that gives due respect and deference to authority figures. *Tarof*, elaborate ceremonial courtesies, determine formal expressions of courtesy, kindness, and hospitality. To say *tarof nist* (it is not tarof) is a genuine expression of courtesy and kindness. Tarof seems to reflect Iran's long ruler-subject political system; it is replete with terms such as *bandeh* or slave.[27]

The certainty of uncertainty has been an integral part of the Iranian social experience.[28] As one writer has observed: "By its very nature, the Iranian value system in providing for diverse circumstances permits the individual considerable flexibility in his behavior. Iranian culture does not condemn man for resorting to trickery to deceive the government or others who have traditionally robbed him of his possessions and security."[29] Iran, not unlike other Middle Eastern societies, values cleverness as a positive virtue. As David McClelland has observed in analyzing children's stories in Iran and Turkey, over two-thirds of the stories from Iran have trickery as their main theme, with honor going to the individual who can outwit an opponent.[30]

Unstable administration in Iranian society over the years seems to have encouraged a strong sense of individualism in terms of personal, community, and regional loyalties, since Iranians were left to fend for themselves. Iranian tribes clearly exemplified this strong group loyalty and autonomy. The price of individual and local group loyalties has been the absence of national unity and public spirit. Because the state under the monarchy was identified with a government whose exactions the citizen guarded against, it appears that a national consciousness failed to develop and thrive in Iran.

The individualism that has characterized Iranians is unlike that known to developed societies, in which independence exists side-by-side with a sense of responsibility to others. Iranian individualism has been marked by distrust based on the assumption that all people are in pursuit of personal interests. Consequently, in Iran, it seems that autonomy and individualism have coexisted with little sense of responsibility to others outside the family and friendship group.[31] The Iranian fear of betrayal and insecurity in interpersonal relations seemingly led to the inflexibility and isolation of individuals. Inevitably, cooperation and coordination among individuals and groups has been difficult, and social action that required individual commitment was stultified. This social milieu apparently produced authority patterns that resulted in external submission to superiors, internal rejection of authority, and a hesitancy to take action unless ordered, plus an obtrusive absence of individual initiative. The sole surviving source of security, cooperation, trust, and succor in Iranian society has been the family. It is reflective of the nature of Iranian society that most homes are surrounded by high walls. It was only within these walls that Iranians "escaped" the isolation and insecurity existing beyond the walls, thereby separating themselves from the world outside.

Socialization and the Iranian Family

As the bridge between generations, the Iranian family has been a primary source of socialization, preparing children for the vicissitudes of Iranian life. The family reflects the value patterns that exist in Iranian society at large. The extended family plays an important role in the life of individuals. The family has been first of all a haven of security and, based on the power of one's extended family, was of significance in determining position and status in society. The family has been the most stable social unit in Iran, and Iranians have derived support and respect from it throughout life.

In the autocratic atmosphere of prerevolutionary Iran, with its pressures and controls, the family served as a place of refuge and solace, particularly for male members of the family. Patrilineal descent has been the norm, with the family organized around men. The Iranian family has traditionally been authoritarian in nature. Although men tended to build a wall, visible and invisible, around the family, it has been in actuality an extended family situation since relatives on both sides and close friends are included, with others excluded. Continuous reciprocal obligations among family members are expected. Within such an environment, individual behavior reflects on family and kin.

Not unlike the larger society with its stress on an ethical, authoritarian way of life, communication in the Iranian family almost always has been one-dimensional—from the dominant to the submissive. In a paternalistic position of unchallengeable authority, the Iranian father makes the major decisions for the family, and discipline is an indispensable tool of training. The child finds security and strength in the relationship to the key figure of the father, who elicits respect and obedience mingled with fear. The Iranian mother, with whom the young child spends much time, develops the gentler side of his or her nature, and acts as intermediary and mediator between husband and children. During the first four to five years, the Iranian mother is the primary nurturing figure in the child's life. It is her responsibility to teach social behavior, in which respect for father and elders is of prime importance. During these years, the father remains in the background, but he looms large in the child's mind, as the child witnesses the respect mother extends to father. Thus, the father is perceived as a source of physical and moral strength and wisdom. The father enters more actively into the child's life at the age of five to six years, especially with male children. Respect for and fear of the father seems to precipitate the process of identification.[32]

In relationship to the rest of the family (other than the father), a son is allowed free expression. As the center of attention, he gains a certain degree of independence and self-assertiveness. But the overriding authority of the father, often arbitrary, places the child in an ambivalent position of being dependent upon the father, while exerting his will with the rest of the family.

The socialization process within the family reflected in miniature the functioning of the ruler-subject political system and those who administered it, particularly in terms of the arbitrary and authoritarian measures of the dominant patrimonial figure, the father. It might be speculated that submission to authority, respect for superiors, rigid control, and the tendency to look upward for direction (and sometimes protection) that have characterized the familial structure in Iran extended into other areas of society, namely, relations between government and the governed. In analyzing the political culture of Ireland, David E. Schmitt makes the following observation, which seems applicable to Iranian political culture up to the time of the Islamic Revolution of 1978–79: "Trust, obedience, and deference toward the male head of one's family, toward the elderly and toward the clergy predisposed Irishmen to accept the decisions of political authority."[33]

As the most stable social unit in Iranian society, the family has provided support for the individual throughout life, and identification and loyalty have been granted first to family and close friends, rather than to groups or group ideals. Unlike the value system inherent in Iranian culture at large, in which circumvention has been an accepted norm, relations within the family and with friends call for honesty and sincerity.

"Personalism refers to a pattern of social relations in which people are valued for who they are and whom they know—not solely for what technical qualifications they possess. Where extreme personalism exists, family and friends determine one's chances for success."[34] Extreme personalism in this sense has characterized Iranian society. The extended family, with its network of personal ties, provided the mechanism for maneuverability in pursuing social and political goals. Family and friendship ties were the preferred channels in business, in employment, and in seeking political favors; reciprocity for favors received was expected. The family served as a stepping stone for individuals within the social system and had an effect on how they related to that system. The political affairs of Iran under the monarchical system were steeped in nepotism, an integral part of the Iranian governmental bureaucracy and a determinant in the selection and advancement of personnel. A great majority of the governmental elite under the late Shah had fathers in government service. It was common practice for the Shah to give provincial governorships and other high administrative posts to family members. Iran was frequently called the country of 1,000 families; the political system was dominated by a limited number of family groups, the political elite of Iran, that maintained proximity to the Pahlavi family.[35]

The novel *Identity Card*, written by Fereidoun Esfandiary, lucidly relates the personalistic nature of the late Shah's governmental apparatus; who you knew determined success or failure, whether in terms of career or merely in accomplishing a minor transaction, such as securing a government-issued identification card.[36] By performing a special service for a member of the family or for a close friend, individuals could expect to receive something in return when needed. When all personal ties failed to achieve an end, Iranians could turn to the time-worn and sanctioned practice of bribery.

As we have seen thus far in this section, position and status in Iranian society were not achieved, but were generally ascribed through personal ties to family and friends; this personal network played a major role in determining one's place in the sociopolitical system. It was not uncommon for an individual to hold several positions at once, with connections and representation in many areas. The Western ideal of the self-made man has not existed in Iran. The Iranian family served as a pillar of veracity, security, and stability within a sociopolitical system that offered no such guarantees, but was marked instead by corruption and arbitrary rule from above. Within the family, Iranians escaped the rivalry and conflict that accompanied the manipulation and opportunism of the larger social system.

Also, the Iranian family has been a microcosm of the macrocosmic sociopolitical system that existed for centuries, particularly in regard to authority patterns. There are marked similarities between familial and governmental organization and behavior patterns: that is, arbitrary authority with power emanating from a central patrimonial figure. In the family this role was performed by the father. Prior to the Islamic Revolution, it was the role of the monarch; in postrevolutionary Iran, it is the Vali-ye-faqih, or Ayatollah Khumayni. Discipline, control, and obedience were stressed in both the family and political system. As one observer writes regarding traditional authority models in Iranian society, "The demand for submission to authority figures seems to be a cultural pattern in Iran: first submission to God, . . . then to the leader of the nation, to those who hold a position higher than oneself and finally, to the authoritarian parent."[37]

The internal struggle of Iranian youth in terms of authority is reflected in James Bill's observation that "he is a young man and an old man."[38] The young are the product of a new age, but concomitantly living within the authoritarian framework of the past. External influences of modernization implied new freedoms and mores, but long-standing social norms insisted upon observance of traditional patterns of authority and behavior in general. Young Iranians were caught between two worlds, old and new. In addition, they were immersed in a political system that demanded the same submission to authority which sought to modernize but relied upon traditional methods of personalism and similar means to maintain control. Old methods were used by the Pahlavi regime to attain new goals; the young were denied a voice in their future in the sociopolitical system, and political development was virtually nullified.

One of the ostensible consequences of modernization in Iran was the erosion of the extended family and the shift, though gradual, to a more nuclear family unit. In addition, authority patterns were slowly attenuated, with the emergence of youth as a "distinct social category."[39] This alteration of authority patterns was reflected in the fact that Iranian youth became more actively engaged in politics and public affairs. Unlike the past, there appeared to be an enhanced need for participation among the young. The emergence of youth as a distinct category was important, for it had implications not only within the family but in the political arena in general.[40] In the Revolution of 1978–79, Iranian youth challenged political authority by taking to the streets in open rebellion against authority.

As seen thus far, authoritarianism and personalism have prevailed in the Iranian family. Within the family, the father is the unrivaled leader, and his word is heeded. The familial patterns described here essentially paralleled the traditional structure of monarchical government in Iran. Since there were no prescribed rules and regulations or accepted administrative procedures to serve as guides to political action, the personal whim of certain individuals, especially the monarch and his minions, determined events in the Iranian political process.

The monarchical-autocratic nature of the state and its resultant despotism created a situation in which the individual's relation to the state was always looser than in the West. Because of the nature of the state, submission to political authority was a requisite to survival. But the extent to which individuals considered themselves members of their state was minimized by the fact that government was identified with exactions; it was essentially an authority to guard against. In such an informal and arbitrary environment, Iranians found integration and identification within the family and its extended network rather than the larger sociopolitical system. Like religion, the communal and family bonds have been stronger than the political bond in Iran. More often than not the individual was able to satisfy needs through a personal network rather than through the political apparatus. The fact that the political system was less than effective in providing formal channels for citizens to accomplish and satisfy certain needs was an important factor in the weak bond between polity and government that existed in the monarchical past.

As noted, the family provided the only bastion of trust and confidence in Iranian society. Iranians have been taught early that in interpersonal relations they cannot be assured of the meaning of—or count

on—the behavior of others. From this insecurity and uncertainty in social relations, young Iranians learned to control and often to mask their
own thoughts. They learned to be guarded in interpersonal relations,
coming to know truths about others but careful in extending information about themselves. In this way they remained in control of relationships. It might be speculated that, given the lack of selfless social action
and cooperative interpersonal relations, an authoritarian relationship
between strong leader and willing follower was a prerequisite for sociopolitical action in Iranian society in the past.

Iranians have been extremely chary about asserting initiative, finding it safer to follow established routines. Also, they have been cautious
in commitment to social action. In the twentieth century, Iranians made
such a commitment, in the Constitutional Revolution, during oil nationalization in the 1950s, and finally with the deposition of the Shah in
1979. Among other factors, the fact that group structure was poorly developed in Iran mitigated against continuance of what had been
achieved earlier during a time of crisis and upheaval. This was particularly clear during the Constitutional Revolution. Once goals were
achieved, the absence of group solidarity and initiative proved detrimental to the persistence of attainments and to the implementation of
an effective constitutional style of government. The absence of cooperation and national unity has been a contributing factor in the formidable
and unwieldy process of putting the government of Iran together after
the Islamic Revolution. But despite internal disunity and strong individualism, solidarity has been achieved at times in Iran based on a disdain
for foreign intrusion into the affairs of the country and upon a surfeit of
governmental corruption. Potent sociopolitical action and national feeling have occurred when Iranians felt a threat from powerful external
entities, as during the constitutional era, the 1950s, and the revolutionary period (1978–79) in which prodigious numbers of people throughout Iran demanded the deposition of the Shah and an end to foreign
penetration into the political and economic life of the country.

The notion of participation by the polity in the political process was
missing in prerevolutionary Iran. This is evinced by the fact that the
concept of citizenship, in the Western sense, does not exist in Persian.
The equivalent for this concept in Persian is *tabi'yat*, which essentially
means follower or dependent. Historically, the sociopolitical process in
Iran revolved around bargaining and mutual favors, with little in the
way of common effort to achieve common objectives.

It should be noted that although the physical arrangement of the family experienced a degree of change from extended to nuclear family, the sociopolitical demands and supports continued basically unchanged. Membership in a family group affected one's power and position in society; these personal ties facilitated advancement and influence. Interest aggregation and articulation were manifested through informal groups such as the family. Thus far we have seen that the family served as a base of support, security, and social status and that Iranians have derived a sense of identity and have learned authority patterns from the family.

A people finds security and expression in a number of protective mechanisms. In Iran the family has fulfilled this purpose. Another protective and expressive device in Iranian society has been a long tradition of speculative thinking and artistic creation, a major ingredient in the value and identity cohesion of Iranian society.

The Intellectual Tradition and National Consciousness

"The most striking feature of the Persians as a nation is their passion for metaphysical speculation. This passion, so far from being confined to the learned classes, permeates all ranks. . . ."[41] Iranians have expressed a spirit of independence over the ages in creative ways. Through literature, Iranian artists not only gave permanence to ideas but also created a basis for national unity and self-consciousness. The rich cultural heritage and common language expressed primarily in poetry have given the Iranian people a sense of pride and superiority, particularly over foreigners. Regarding the contribution of poets to the development of culture in Iran, Reza Arasteh asserts that "when some of them sought to recapture the glories of past epochs they succeeded in immortalizing both history and themselves."[42]

Literature, especially those themes expressed by Iran's beloved poets, through the ages has influenced the thinking of all classes: the literate through reading, and the masses through memorization and recitation of poetical works. Every Iranian knows the *Shahnameh* (Chronicle of kings) of Ferdowsi,[43] which poetically recounts the history of Iran from creation of man to the end of the Sassanian dynasty and emphasizes the perennial glory of Iran and its legendary heroes. The power of creative expression, and specifically that of Ferdowsi, is best expressed by an observer who writes: "By indicating the pattern of renewal from age to age of the strength and glory of the nation, he held out the promise of renaissance to the people of later centuries when the country had fallen on bad times. It is through the *Shahnama* that even the illiterate peasant identifies himself with a national entity."[44] It is through literature, especially poetry, that Iranians join with their fellows, of all gradations in society, in a common understanding and a social spirit that is timeless.

The literary tradition in Iran has tended to unite the Iranian people, giving them a sense of pride and national identification. It has also been a conduit of social and political protest in a land where such outlets have been few and far between. In addition, the desire for a principled existence is expressed through Iranian literature and poetry.

It is in the abstract medium of literature and poetry that the Iranian temperament is best understood. On one hand, the Iranian cultural tradition and the experience of a people were unfolded through poetry about Iran's supremacy and the glory of its kings. On the other hand, contemporary Iranian poetry evoked a sense of sadness and anger over a political condition the individual felt helpless to control. The spirit of revolt and search for national identity are revealed in the poem "That Which Isn't Mine" by Ahmad Shamlu (penname Bamdad), written during the reign of Mohammad Reza Pahlavi:

> I am bothered by a pain
>   which isn't mine,
> I have lived in a land
>   which isn't mine,
> I have lived with a name
>   which isn't mine,
> I have wept of grief
>   which isn't mine,
> I was born out of joy
>   which isn't mine,
> I die of a death
>   which isn't mine.*

Contemporary Iranian poetry evinced the vacuum felt by society, particularly its youth, in terms of identification with the political system

---

*This poem in Persian is in Ahmad Shamlu's *Bāgh-i Ayena* (Mirror of a Garden), Tehran: Morevareed, 1336/1957, p. 65, and translated by A. Reza Arasteh in his book *Man and Society in Iran*, Leiden: E. J. Brill, 1970, p. 188. Permission to reprint courtesy of E. J. Brill.

and the changes that took place under the Pahlavi regime. The lack of citizen participation and decision making in the political process was reflected in poetical themes, often related through the use of metaphors, subtleties, and an esoteric writing style. Under the Pahlavi regime, artistic endeavor was strangled by official government censorship.[45]

A contradiction has existed in Iran regarding such virtues as honesty and sincerity; although a respect and admiration for such virtues has existed, there has been a reticence to display and practice them publicly. One reason for this seems to be that social advancement required cautious behavior and, at times, surreptitious conduct on the part of the polity. Consequently, the expression of true convictions was hampered. Although admired, these virtues seemed to be anomalous in the sociopolitical system. Commitment to ideas and ideals manifested in the Iranian literary tradition was a necessary ingredient to preserve a principled existence in a system where commitment and straightforward behavior were generally moot, except in the context of the family.

Finally, the inveterate individualism of the Iranian people is expressed in the original thought of its poets and philosophers. In a society where individual initiative was generally considered inefficacious and often dangerous to one's position in the community and where submission to superiors was the norm, the printed and spoken word was an important vehicle of individual expression. In monarchical Iran, where political opposition was denied a voice, literature and poetry served as an instrument for dissent. The influence of Iranian poets on the thought and speech of the ordinary Iranian is unique. Even the most "illiterate" Iranian can quote from the great poets, such as Sadi, Hafez, Ferdowsi, Rumi, and others.

The national feeling that springs from the literary tradition in Iran is in itself an interesting phenomenon. Although much of Iran's literature exults in a glorious past and seems to have produced a fierce pride in Iranian culture and civilization, there was no commensurate attachment to the political system that ruled over the nation. The national feeling evinced in the poetry of Iran was not axiomatically transferred to the nation's political system. The literature of Iran evoked instead a kind of cultural nationalism.

Iran can be characterized as a nation imbued with "an unusually distinguished and persistent intellectual tradition. The cultivation of the mind has always been encouraged and honored in Iran."[46] The role of this intellectual tradition in shaping a national idea and national identity cannot be overlooked. In light of the many divisive factors in Iranian society, the people's pride in Iran's history, expressed through literature, has served as a cohesive force. This sense of pride contributed to the endurance of Iranian identity and feelings of uniqueness in times of invasion and turmoil and has been a base in which all strata of society find a common identification. The Iranian literary tradition fostered a cultural consciousness by transmitting this tradition from one generation to the next. When the late Shah's censorship became too extreme, Iran's poets and writers masked their dissatisfaction with the political system in metaphors and subtleties. The Iranian literary tradition has contributed to the development of a cultural nationalism that has aided in the preservation of national identity through the ages.

Education and Socialization

Although the literary tradition manifests Iranian individualism and independence, the educational process was aimed at making the individual into an obedient member of the family and society in general. The emphasis of education in the West is to make the individual as independent as possible, whereas in Iran the socialization process centered around instilling a sense of obedience in children so that they would follow the rules of elders and subordinate their interests to persons of authority.

The traditional Iranian system of education consisted of maktabs, a system of religious schools supported by private contributions and religious foundations, which were frequently associated with a mosque.[47] The maktab emphasized reading, writing, and familiarity with the Quran, with stress on religion and moral training. Classical texts such as Sadi's *Gulistan* and the poems of Hafez and Ferdowsi were part of the curriculum, with religion and moral training predominant. The *maktab-dar* (teacher) taught in a rote manner, emphasizing memorization of material and maintenance of discipline.

For centuries, education was a religious and family affair, with formal teaching strictly in the hands of mullahs. It was not until the beginning of the twentieth century that emphasis changed, with the central government taking an active part in education. During the rule of Reza Shah, the principle of state direction of education was instituted.[48] Although it remained an integral part of the curriculum, religion was no longer the strongest component in Iranian education; rather, the educational system became a tool of Reza Shah's brand of nationalism. It is important to note that, although secular education was introduced, this did not alter the basic belief that the educational process was to be involved in teaching morality. Ethics and morality were not separated from the essential "fact" learning of secular education. The link between knowledge and morality in Iranian education was never broken, merely transformed.

Although secular education became the goal of the Pahlavi regime, religion continued as a substantial force in Iranian education. It is interesting that the message of religious stories was often obliquely political. The following extract is from the elementary school readers of fifth and sixth grade classes in Iran. Superficially, the story revolves around the tragedy and martyrdom of Imam Hossein, but its political message cannot be dismissed:

> Imam Hossein did not accept *sitamgari* [oppression] and *zulm* [injustice], and he did not take the advice of those who wanted him to be silent or cooperate with Yazid. For Muslims, *Sayyid al-Shuhadas' qiyam-i mardanah* [the Prince of Martyrs' intrepid insurrection] gave renewed spirit to the people. His *shahadat* [martyrdom] at Karbala served as a model of resistance against *sitamgari*. Imam Hossein said many times, "I see life under a *sitamgar* [oppressor] to be *khastah khunandah* [enervating] and *na-rava* [unjust], and I would be gladdened to leave this world." Also, at the site of battle, when he had lost all his friends and was left alone to face the enemy, he said, "We will never conspire with *sitamgaran* [oppressors]."[49]

Because of the administrative needs of the Pahlavi bureaucracy, the Iranian educational system was transformed to produce morally oriented statesmen. Although other subjects composed the curriculum in universities, stress was on Iranian literature, poetry, and morality. The same was true of the curriculum of secondary schools, which included history, geography, and general science, with emphasis upon mastery of Iranian culture and language expressed through literature and poetry.[50] The educational process has been one of imparting information, rather than developing and encouraging independent, critical thinking habits on the part of students.

Education prior to the twentieth century centered around religious instruction. But the objective of the Ministry of Education under the Pahlavi regime was to train students to become "productive" members of society.[51] What this meant to the Pahlavi regime was best expressed in the words of Prime Minister Amir Abbas Hoveyda in a personal interview on 29 May 1967: "The Iranian student must be courageous and willing to sacrifice. He should and can form student unions and organizations. He should not, however, build these into anything political. That is not his business."[52] The Ministry of Education under Mohammad Reza Pahlavi controlled all aspects of education: finance, personnel, curriculum, supervision, construction, and the like. State control of schools reached into the private schools as well, since they were required to use official textbooks and follow the official course of study.

Beginning with the regime of Reza Shah, the stress was on higher education, sacrificing long-range investment for immediate needs. What began as a push to fulfill the immediate bureaucratic personnel needs of government administration in the late 1920s and 1930s metamorphosed into a political policy of preservation. Through policies of assimilation of Iranian youth into the governmental apparatus, the regime was in a better position to control them as a group. Whereas in the 1930s a college education was a luxury reserved for upper-class and government-sponsored youth, this privilege was extended to the middle class after World War II. The regime's rationale for including the middle class in the ranks of the higher educated was eventually to assimilate them into the ranks of government, thereby reducing the possibility of dissent from this segment of society. Industry and business had not developed to the point where they could absorb the college trained; in order to circumvent their dissatisfaction with government, the policy of recruiting Iranian youth into the governmental system was initiated, thereby creating economic dependence upon the state and submission to political authority. As one writer noted regarding the establishment of the University of Tehran, "the bureaucracy was continually expanded to meet the vocational aspirations of the graduates."[53] In essence, the ever-expanding bureaucracy developed as a mechanism to preserve the status quo, furthering state control. A degree and family and social connections were the criteria to gain a position in government.[54]

As it developed, the Pahlavi government became the major source of potential employment for educated youth, with university graduates automatically expecting government employment. Of course, this resulted in a swollen bureaucracy. The Pahlavi government, in order to thwart the frustration of youth who might vent political dissatisfaction in the streets, attempted to absorb Iran's educated into the political system. A "good" educational system to the political authority of the time was one that reinforced its authority and a "bad" educational system was one that weakened the Shah's political control.

The Iranian education system, like the larger society, emphasized obedience to authority, and with this rigid control came a dependence on direction from above. It has been the student's duty to learn and excel, not to challenge authority. The submissive nature of the educational process seems to have played a part in the political culture of Iran. Monarchical authority was not unnatural in a social system well acquainted with obedience to authority from above.

SUMMARY

From this analysis of the social structure of Iranian society, authoritarianism and personalism in social relations are clear. Obedience and deference to authority learned early in the family and the educational system predisposed Iranians to accept the decisions of authority at large and political authority in particular. The personalism of social relations evolved into a sociopolitical system in which people were valued and success was based on who they were and whom they knew. In the Iranian social milieu of ascribed status, family and friends determined one's position, advancement, and effectiveness in society.

In analyzing the politics of Iran in terms of its social structure, it might be concluded that it has been the domain of individuals rather than groups. It is interesting to note that the Tudeh party, which proved to be an unsustaining force in Iranian politics, was a party of ideas rather than personalities, emphasizing group policies and goals. On the other hand, the National Front party, a lively force in Iranian politics from the 1950s on, was a party of charismatic individuals, such as Mossadegh and Kashani. Mossadegh in particular was the epitome of a paternalistic, yet strong leader. In addition, he espoused antiforeign sentiments and was seen as an honest man by his numerous supporters, which made him all the more appealing to the Iranian people. Through his brand of personal leadership, Mossadegh became the symbol of Iranian nationalism in the 1950s. Mossadegh's age, honesty, charisma, intellectualism, and paternalistic authority—admired characteristics in Iranian culture, especially for political leaders—accounted for his popularity and political power.

One of the most striking examples of this idea of authority and personality is Ayatollah Khumayni, leader of the Islamic Republic of Iran. His image is that of a charismatic and strong leader. Khumayni's asceticism wards off suspicion of corruption and connotes a refusal to be seduced by materialism and power. His intrepid confrontation with more powerful nations suggests strength and authority, plus the important element of guarding the nation from foreign intrusion. Ayatollah Khumayni cleverly combined political and religious leadership. His persona, reflecting important cultural images, has had much to do with his sustained leadership in the midst of political divisiveness.

Traditionally, Iranians have looked to a strong leader to provide guardianship of the national sovereignty. The paternal relationship between the ruler and his subjects that dominated the political realm of Iran for centuries was a reflection of the microcosmic family relationship, in which the authority of the father has been absolute. In the absence of formal rules and laws, the dictates of the ruler dominated. Rule from above with little, if any, input from below has been a cultural variable of the family as well as the traditional political culture in general. Although Iranians inherently distrust power, they historically looked to a strong leader in times of turmoil. As in the microcosmic family, where the father's role is protection of his family, the expected role of the national leader is the protection of the empire, especially from external threats that would deprive the nation of its independence.

One of the most important elements that enables a political system to create viable and effective organizations and institutions to deal with rising demands and to confront political and administrative needs is the ability of citizens to cooperate. The high walls surrounding Iranian homes have been a symbol of the exclusiveness of individuals within the social setting of family and disconnection from the monarchical political system of the past. Clubs and social organizations, common in the West, have been a rarity in Iran. The focus of social activity is the family.

Association outside the family has been difficult to achieve in a society such as Iran, imbued with distrust and suspicion, where dictatorial and arbitrary rule was the norm of sociopolitical life for centuries. It might be said that arbitrary rule from above numbed the potential for association and cooperation among Iranians, minimizing organizational skills and inhibiting the capacity for leadership as well as the ability to follow. The authoritarian political system of Iran seems to have had another effect; it has made Iranians wary of authority, and at times it has made them reject the oppressiveness of the system.

The issue of individualism and association is not restricted merely to Iran, but seems to be a condition of the Middle East in general, affecting political institutions in the area:

> Political associations as important and effective action units have been
> conspicuously absent in the social history of the Islamic Middle East.
> Institutional groups hold a more central position in the Middle Eastern
> political history than do associational collectives. . . . Institutional groups
> in the Middle East have tended to be large sprawling conglomerates of per-
> sonal cliques, familial networks, and regional factions.[55]

The lack of formal group structure has been one factor in the dearth of
political development in Iran, in that the political system was unable to
institutionalize new patterns of organization and procedures to deal
with the political and administrative needs of the country. This was particularly distressing in a country that faced the ever-increasing demands
brought on by the late Shah's modernization. Interest articulation and
aggregation were ultimately expressed through informal groups, con-
glomerations of personal cliques, familial networks, and regional factions. This dispersion and fragmentation of interest through informal
groups mitigated against the development of viable organizational and
institutional structures that, if allowed to develop, would carry out the
business and decision-making processes of the country. The absence of
organizational rationale and structure created a situation in which
"structure after structure—family, village, clan, class, sect, army, party,
elite, state—turns out, when more narrowly looked at, to be an *ad hoc*
constellation of miniature systems of power, a cloud of unstable micro-
politics, which compete, ally, gather strength, and, very soon overex-
tended, fragment again."[56]

With each group, or individual, seeking to protect certain interests
and achieve certain goals, there was continual flux among all units. Although such a system fostered a certain fluidity and flexibility essentially
missing in a more formal structure, the ephemeral nature of institutional groups mitigated against the development of organizational cohesiveness and efficiency, a requisite for a modern state. Regarding
political evolution in the developing world, Pye comments:

> The development of effective organizations depends fundamentally upon
> the capacity of individuals to associate with each other. This capacity calls
> into question a wide range of basic human values and the ability of indi-
> viduals to make commitments—commitments as to the goals and pur-
> poses of group action, the means and spirit of associational relationships,
> the appropriate limits of such associations and the integrity of self. . . .[57]

In order for government to thrive and develop, a substantial degree of public support and loyalty is required. Traditionally, channels to power have been informal, and Iranians generally placed their loyalties and trust in such channels. Loyalty to clan took precedence over loyalty to the political system. A necessary element to ensure participation in a group goal is that individuals be convinced that their efforts will make a notable difference in pursuing the group's interest. The conspicuous absence of formal institutions with well-defined principles of goal attainment in prerevolutionary Iran reflected the fact that the informal group structure was perceived as a more effective channel to pursue sociopolitical goals.

Personalism in relations has been a pronounced feature of Iranian political culture. It has been a pervasive fact of life in Iran, dominating in family, occupational, educational, and political settings. As James Bill points out, "Power has not flowed from institution to institution but rather from individual to individual."[58] In such a system, personal relationships and ties were critically important in terms of access to power. Since power was centralized in individuals rather than in institutions, success—and often survival—depended upon networks of personal contacts and the ability to use them. Loyalty, when confined to personal ties of family and clan, limits the development of a sense of responsibility and integration with members of the same political system.

One of the duties of the political system is to provide for its members, which is essential to system preservation. The cultural context is an important factor government must consider in deciding what will be provided to members of the polity. The policy of rapid modernization undertaken by Mohammad Reza Pahlavi displayed a blatant disregard of Iranian culture. Iran is a country steeped in tradition, where religion, family, and the arts are most important to the people. Modernization in the style of the West strained these cultural entities.

The absence of formal structures in the political system was detrimental to the practice of government in Iran under the late Shah. The cooperation and association necessary to effective administration have traditionally been nonexistent in the Iranian political apparatus. With the removal of the monarch as the central ruling authority, it became quite evident that these variables play a dominant role in putting the political system on its feet. For centuries Iranians have survived within the sociopolitical milieu of dominance; it will be difficult to look within rather than up for authority. New political culture values and behaviors will be needed to evolve a less authoritarian, more participatory form of government in Iran. It appears that in order to create a functional, diverse political system, old patterns of political socialization—authoritarianism, elitism, personalism, individualism—must undergo transformation, giving way to new norms conducive to a self-governing political system in which power is shared rather than centralized in one individual and an elite.

Using the cultural constructs presented thus far, the last two chapters focus on the old and new political systems of Iran. By analyzing the governmental process under the late Shah, we can derive a clearer understanding of the forces that moved the country to the Islamic Revolution of 1978–79.

V

Authority and Power: The Reign of Mohammad Reza Pahlavi (1953-78)

For 2,500 years the Iranian political system was characterized by the absolute authority of the monarch. This tradition of prodigious authority from above was balanced by the Iranian people's inherent suspicion and often resentment of political authority. While not active participants in the political process as understood in the West, because of the monarch's absolute power Iranians learned to be politically astute in perceiving political authority. The indigenous distrust of political authority by the polity bred skepticism and reluctance to give enduring allegiance to a national leader.

Recent history evidences Iranian distrust and disdain of political authority pushed to its breaking point. The twentieth century marks an evolutionary movement toward the eventual demise of traditional government in Iran. This revolutionary flow began circa 1900 with the push for constitutional government and the lessening of monarchical authority. It arose again in the early 1950s with the shift in power, although temporary, from the monarchy to a popular prime minister, Mossadegh, who attempted to limit the power of the throne and rid the country of foreign intervention. The evolution reached its zenith in the

Revolution of 1978–79 when Mohammad Reza Pahlavi was overthrown by the will of the Iranian people. During the two earlier periods the Iranian people were given the opportunity to experiment in free expression and social organization, leading ultimately to the expression of their desire for freedom from monarchical tyranny and absolutism. But in this century the political process in Iran was marked by the omnipresent and imperious role of the Pahlavi monarchy. As James Bill so keenly observes regarding the Pahlavi regime, "The half century of Pahlavi monarchy in Iran has been characterized by traditional patterns in which the Shah promotes passive servitude in all relationships that others maintain toward him and balanced rivalry in all other personal, group, and class interaction. . . ."[1]

This chapter examines the structure of Iranian politics as conducted for twenty-five years by Mohammad Reza Pahlavi. The political process followed by the last of the Pahlavi monarchs shows how the seeds of revolution were sown during this epoch. Finally, this chapter examines Iran's ruler-subject political system vis-à-vis the dominant cultural variables outlined thus far.

ERA OF SUPREME AUTHORITY

As we have seen, rapid upward mobility has occurred at times in Iranian history. One such example is the rise of the Pahlavis, who descended from a line of undistinguished military officers from the province of Mazandaran, acquiring power through armed force.

Government under Mohammad Reza Pahlavi involved the amalgamation of authority in the hands of a supreme ruler. The Shah was the sole policymaker in Iran. Government policy and action had as its main criterion the preservation and strengthening of the Shah's and his family's power, the survival of the monarchical institution, and the goal of building the power of the Iranian state. While leaving the details of administration to closely watched functionaries, the Shah monopolized the dynamics of politics in Iran, carefully orchestrating political socialization and recruiting potential opponents into his bureaucracy. The Shah's power was derived mainly from the army, the bureaucracy, and the United States government. After the Shah reclaimed the throne in 1953, support from the United States bought time to develop his mainstays of support, specifically the army and gendarmerie, which were rewarded handsomely for their loyalty. In 1954, the Shah began the process of reestablishing the throne as the center of authority. Thus began the era of royal dictatorship and government based on sustaining the Shah's power. From the year of Mossadegh's overthrow through the 1960s, the Shah moved steadily to tighten his authority over society; this was done with American economic aid.[2]

The Shah's forced departure from the national scene in 1953 led to his rethinking of previous policy. His new bulwark of power was the military and security apparatus he developed. Under the Shah's personal direction, a monolithic security system was created, including intelligence forces, town and city police, country gendarmerie, royal guardsmen (the Immortals), and a large military establishment. The Imperial Inspectorate was created in 1958 and was answerable to no one but the Shah. All government agencies were ordered to cooperate with this investigative body, which carried out regular, unannounced inspections. Its function was to monitor how ministries and individuals carried out the Shah's policies, checking on loyalty and misconduct in government circles. Its control extended over and above the SAVAK, and its command was drawn largely from the military. The military hierarchy was a privileged group in Iranian society enjoying fringe benefits, modern facilities, the newest equipment, and priorities in terms of military requests. All promotions above the rank of major were personally approved by the Shah.[3]

The Shah's forced departure also led to a twofold policy of divide and rule and the absorption of challenging groups and individuals into the bureaucracy. His policy of divide and rule was based on the distribution of power to select individuals or agencies with overlapping functions intended to keep these forces fragmented and basically impotent. The political system that developed was founded on mutual antagonism and distrust. In the political apparatus devised by the Shah there appeared to be a constitutional side, but along with this was, as Robert Graham observes, a covert unconstitutional side:

> The former consists of what would seem in a Western society the institutions of democracy: the Prime Minister's office and the Cabinet; the Majles; the single political party, Rastakhiz; the provincial governors and the press. However, the functions of these are either controlled, monitored or duplicated by the covert side which consists of the Imperial Inspectorate, SAVAK, the armed forces, military tribunals, powerful individuals without fixed positions and the economic power of the Royal Family. . . . Thus the exercise of power has come to depend exclusively upon the Shah's relationships with a series of individuals either in their function as heads of agencies and Ministries or as individuals.[4]

With his security system strengthened and encouraged in its loyalty to him, the Shah turned in 1957 to the nascent middle class for a government with greater public appeal and dependence on the state, co-opting opponents into his political elite and bureaucracy. The government became the major employer for Iranian youth, particularly university graduates. This was perceived as a deterrent to political opposition. Regardless of rational need or economic resources to support the influx of university graduates into the governmental bureaucracy, it was felt that their induction was a necessary method of control to counter political subversion. Not uncommonly, individuals once active in the opposition such as the Tudeh or the National Front became full-fledged members of the political elite and the political bureaucracy.

From 1954 to 1963, the Shah's main preoccupation was with internal security, which led ultimately to the elimination of parliamentary opposition. Two puppet parties replaced the banned political parties: the Melliyun (Nationalist) party and the Mardom (People's) party were led and filled by loyal followers of the Shah. March 1975 saw the demise of the two-party system and the establishment of a single party, the Rastakhiz (Resurgence) party. Opponents of the regime, especially those individuals with links to the National Front and Tudeh parties, were subjected to ruthless suppression. Close surveillance was kept on the ulama as well as the bazaar merchants, suppressing any power that might surface, especially in the bazaar. During 1963, the government faced its greatest opposition, particularly from members of the reorganized National Front party, university students, and religious order. Opposition to the Shah was ultimately suppressed, but only after periods of bloody confrontation on Iran's streets. Ironically, it was in 1964 that Iran's rising political-revolutionary leader, Ayatollah Khumayni, was exiled for his political exhortations against the regime. This turbulent time resulted in total dominance by the political center with the aid of extensive security systems, principally the SAVAK, and the proliferation of an obsequious governmental bureaucracy, with opposition to the regime seeking refuge underground. The Shah relied, like his father, upon the force of his army to reestablish control, but he also used psychological weapons, based on an acute awareness of sociocultural norms, to reassert authority.

Divide and Rule

As chief policymaker, the Shah delegated to his political elite the function of translating his policies and decisions into action. Within the framework he created, the political elite competed for position, power, and proximity to the center of authority.

The administrative system fashioned by Shah Mohammad Reza Pahlavi embodied the elements of personalism, informality, and balanced conflict. The administrative system revolved around the person of the Shah, who manipulated it according to his personal desires and goals. The development of a large organizational framework did not minimize the Shah's role as the key decisionmaker and political protagonist.

Under the Shah's regime, political action was based not on prescribed laws and regulations but on his personal inclinations. Such a political style, with a lack of predictability, produced a government based on survivorship; those enmeshed in it became adept at political machinations and maneuvering in order to survive.[5] Since institutional protection of positions did not exist, commitment—especially to change—was abjured. Prime Minister Hoveyda was a good example of the tenuous position of members of the government. Hoveyda was prime minister from 1966 to August 1977, an obtrusively loyal and subservient member of the Shah's elite throughout. He was cast aside when the Shah found it necessary to respond in some way to the demands made by the intelligentsia and bourgeoisie for greater liberalism. In addition, Hoveyda became the scapegoat for the unpopular policies of the Shah. Innovation and initiative were looked upon as "scene stealing," since this type of action was perceived by the Shah as a political threat; someone with ability might gain popularity with the polity. The Shah generally took credit for ideas and programs. A germane example of this was the land reform program, created in fact by Hasan Arsanjani. Arsanjani was forced to resign as minister of agriculture in March 1963 when he became too popular in rural Iran, where he traveled extensively campaigning for the peasants. He was quickly removed from Iran by being appointed ambassador to Rome. His name was erased from all official publications regarding land reform, thereby, in the Shah's mind, erasing the challenge Arsanjani's popularity might have presented.[6]

Neutrality in government functioning was required of members of the bureaucracy from cabinet members to the lowest clerk. Technical proficiency was not required. Each individual was considered equally competent to fill any position; for example, the minister of education might be shifted to the Ministry of Labor. Seniority was the basic criterion in promotion; quality of performance did not enter in. The role of the cabinet within the Shah's regime is best explicated by a writer who observes:

> The Prime Minister's main task within the Cabinet is to orchestrate a result that has been agreed in advance. The Cabinet makes no important decisions. These are reached in advance by the Shah in private audiences either with the Prime Minister or with individual Ministers or heads of agencies. At best the Cabinet acts as a forum for working out the application of a decision.
>
> The weakness of the Prime Minister, and the Cabinet, stems from the Shah's control over their appointment and dismissal. . . . Damage to the Shah's credibility is the sole effective check on his power of hire and fire.[7]

Under such precarious circumstances it was not unusual to find ministers and other governmental officials extremely defensive in protecting their domain, often to the point of distorting information reaching the Shah in order to receive his approbation. The antagonism and rivalry bred by such attitudes ensured that no member of the political elite gained any significant power that might jeopardize the Shah. It is easy to realize that inefficiency proliferated in such a competitive milieu.

Just as Tehran has been the geographic center of political power, the monarchy was the center of control over the political apparatus, rationing that power at will. Further insecurity within the bureaucracy was fostered by a policy that allowed individuals of the lower echelon to bypass formal channels of communication within the hierarchy and to report directly to the political center. This system allowed the leadership to intervene at any level of the political apparatus and also created the idea that the omnipotent center was available to and concerned with all people no matter what their rank. The traditional hierarchical orientation of Iranian society in which individual initiative and independence were discouraged was reinforced by the Pahlavi regime. Concentration of authority and decision making at the top merely perpetuated administrative avoidance and dependency. The dominant-submissive role learned early in life was transferred to the ruler-subject political system of Iran and utilized efficaciously by the Shah.

Insecurity was an obtrusive characteristic of the Iranian political system because position within it was based not on skill or merit, but rather on the will of the monarch, the main dispenser of favors and position. Regarding the mechanisms for maintenance of the political system that flavored the Pahlavi regime, James Bill comments, "The characteristics of tension, personalism, informality and insecurity which have marked power relationships in Iran have all been interrelated in a manner that has reinforced the traditional system. . . ."[8] The rivalry and competition between individuals and groups promoted by the Shah created a balance of tension sufficient to maintain traditional patterns of rule based on servitude.

The political system under the Shah was based on individuals rather than institutions; and to be successful members of the system, individuals learned how to cope within it and maximize the benefits. In describing Iranian politics during the Shah's regime, one observer points out the essence of the process:

> For politics in Iran does present opportunities for the acquisition of those rewards that are available in Iran, rewards in the Weberian sense of class, status, and political power. Whereas these rewards are conventionally available from alternate areas of human endeavor in other societies, in Iran they emanate almost exclusively from the political process which thus becomes so much more central than other areas.[9]

So it was that politics in Iran was in the hands of one man, the Shah. His monopoly of political power involved interest articulation, political socialization, recruitment, and the like, with administrative functions left to carefully selected and supervised functionaries, whose duties often overlapped, leading to fragmentation and enervation. Monarchical control was not limited to civil authorities but included other bodies such as the press, whose function was that of a subservient arm of the government. In addition, the judiciary was completely absorbed into the executive, with military courts usurping the power of this public body. The balance of tension based on mistrust was established monarchical policy, intended to preserve power.

As in the larger social system of Iran, in which individualism has been based on autonomy without responsibility (that is, individuals have avoided personal commitment to others outside of their primary group), the political system manifested and displayed this cultural variable. The absence of confidence and trust in fellows was a cultural orientation efficacious to the dictatorial political style of the Shah. Iranian individualism obviated the formation of effective group action that might have undermined the central authority. The tension and isolation of individuals and agencies assured their subservience, inefficiency, and lack of political development. One unexpected paradox of this individualism based on a lack of personal commitment, which the government used for its maintenance, was a dearth of personal commitment to the political system itself. When commitment to the political system was crucial to the survival of the central authority during the revolutionary period of the 1970s, it did not exist. This lack can be traced to the Shah's own political policy of divide and rule.

The Shah's style of leadership, wherein all important ideas and strategies appeared to emanate from the throne, led to a situation where he stood alone when dissatisfaction within the society grew to the point of rebellion. He became an ignominious figure and the focal point for all the social and political dissatisfactions and frustrations of the polity.

Power through Co-optation of the Middle Class

Just as the Shah utilized the policy of balanced conflict in his own bureaucracy to mitigate its power in the political apparatus, this same strategy was used among the classes. There are those who believe that the Shah's White Revolution was an attempt to turn the peasants against the professional middle class, thereby preserving the traditional system.[10] Essentially, land reform was intended to rally the peasants on the side of the Shah to counteract the threat of the burgeoning middle class.

The rise of a new professional middle class in Iran occurred because of increased educational opportunities, economic development, and contacts with the West. The professional bureaucratic middle class was distinguishable from the entrepreneurial middle class that had always existed in Iran. This new class was composed of individuals whose power came from employment based upon a modern education. Since their position in society was not based on ownership, they were not of the bourgeoisie.[11] This new class in Iranian society was perceived by the political authority as a force to be reckoned with, not only because of its ever-increasing numbers, but due to its very nature. The socioeconomic position of this sector of society was based not on traditional values of material wealth or property, but on accomplishment resulting from special skills and talent. The loyalty of the professional middle class was troublesome to the Shah, because as a group they had shown antipathy and nonacceptance of traditional power relationships that dominated the structure of government.

The Shah's ambivalence regarding the new middle class was not unfounded; the two major opposition parties—the Tudeh and National Front—were organized, led, and composed of large segments of the professional middle class. It was the intelligentsia who responded in the

1960s to the slight letup of government pressure by organizing full-scale demonstrations and rallies against the government. In 1961, during a demonstration by teachers, a panicked policeman fired and killed one man. The potential for mob violence in Tehran because of this incident led the Shah to dismiss his entire cabinet and appoint Ali Amini, a leading Independent, to mitigate the crisis. Amini played a role in exposing the election scheme of the 1960s in which a two-party system was constructed but candidates were carefully chosen by the Shah. During this period, the University of Tehran became the scene of political demonstrations by students and teachers, leading to commando-type raids by the government on the University in 1962–63 to squelch dissent.[12]

Pacification of the professional middle class became a government priority, with a program of co-optation or bribery of the potential opposition to meet the perceived threat to traditional political authority. Essentially, it consisted of drawing key members of the new class into the traditional political system through occupational, social, and economic incentives. Governmental policy was based on the notion that individuals who accepted these inducements no longer posed a threat to the traditional political patterns. As members of the political system, with a stake in its preservation, individuals would be jeopardizing their own interests by challenging it. At this point it is interesting to note the comments of one observer regarding the machinations of the Shah's state apparatus in response to political challenge: "The political authority, whenever the political threat to itself became paramount, capitulates to the educated and the educator-to-be and further expands both the educational system and the educated political leadership class, regardless of rational need or the availability of economic resources to support the policy."[13] For the Shah's regime, it was a truism that "an educated man with a government position, any government position, no matter how unrewarding, is not a political subversive, and conversely, that an educated man without a government position is apt to be a subversive in the hopes of reversing a political situation unfavorable to himself."[14]

To carry out the Shah's policy of co-optation and control, the absorptive capacity of the political system was expanded, bringing in technically educated Iranians, among other elements of the new middle class. Remunerations were made available to them, but distribution of these rewards was maintained by the Shah, as was control from the political center. Reinforcement was offered to those individuals and classes supportive of traditional patterns, bringing them in closer contact with the apex of power. Whereas in former times political recruitment was restricted to the traditional elite, increased oil revenue and American economic aid opened government to nonaristocratic aspirants, whom the Shah attempted to induct into his political apparatus. Recruitment of this new class was undertaken without alienating the established elite, because the Shah saw to it that the elite retained their positions, while new positions were created for those individuals entering the bureaucracy. Closer proximity to the monarch and power was allowed to the dutiful among the traditional elite, satisfying their material needs, as well as their need for power. The Shah's policy of co-optation seemed to serve another purpose, that of splintering and dissipating the power of the professional middle class. Regardless of rational need, government was enlarged, to the point that it became the major source of employment. Expectation regarding government output in terms of potential employment swelled, as did the bureaucracy. The issue of rising expectations in government employment and other areas in relation to the legitimacy and maintenance of political authority is discussed below. Through his co-optation policy, the Shah was able to control the size and composition of the political system and also to limit the demands, both political and economic, of the polity.

The Shah attempted to assuage the professional middle class by creating an atmosphere of reform and change. His White Revolution (1963) and much-touted land reform served this purpose. The 1963 reform program was to involve land reform; nationalization of forests and pastures; public sale of state-owned factories to finance land reform; profit sharing in industry; reform of electoral laws to include women; creation of the Literacy Corps, Health Corps, Reconstruction and Development Corps, and rural courts of justice; nationalization of waterways; national reconstruction; and education and administrative reforms. In addition, the land reform program encompassed religiously endowed lands, a major source of religious revenue. For many, land reform seemed to serve the purpose of suppressing religious opposition.[15] Rationalization for succumbing was made easier by the introduction of revolutionary jargon to characterize government modernization programs.

The White Revolution was intended to stabilize the monarchy and centralize government control. The upheaval of the 1960s showed that large numbers of the professional middle class refused to relate to the dominant system of political authority. The disquiet of the 1960s gave impetus to a governmental policy of strengthening relations with those classes that historically supported the monarchy. To balance and counteract the perceived threat from the professional middle class, the Shah sought to gain the support of the peasant masses. Land reform was limited in scope because it was based on the premise that social change must never undermine the institutions and values that supported the position of the political authority. Land reform diminished somewhat the Shah's reliance on landlords, a powerful group whose support was required in the past. The economic condition of the 1960s created new opportunities for the elite to amass wealth, for many diversified their holdings to include urban land and real estate, commerce, light industry, and foreign securities. Regarding the outcome of the Shah's land reform policies, one writer avers:

> While disassociated from land-based wealth, however, the landlords do become more dependent on these other sources of riches. And those sources of wealth in turn tend to be directly controlled by the government. That is, the land reform has not destroyed the financial power of this one segment of society—no social revolution has been effected. Rather, land reform has altered the importance of the elite's sources of wealth (and ultimately their bases of political power) to those that are under the control of the government.[16]

Through the land reform program, both landowners and peasants suffered a diminution of their former independence while the central political authority amassed greater control over their lives and fortunes. For landowners-turned-entrepreneurs, the political authority was able to exert control through a plethora of regulations relating to commercial and industrial processes, requiring the intervention of government ministries. Also, the power base that assured the election of landlords to parliament was eroded by land reform, thereby increasing the Shah's control over the Majlis. Prior to land reform, landowners were able to galvanize the votes of peasants who occupied their lands and villages and were guaranteed election to parliament; consequently, landowners controlled this body. Land reform truncated this political link between landlords and peasant voters (65 percent of the population) and gave the Shah greater control over the electoral process and the Majlis. He had previously attempted to exert control over the Majlis through a number of devices. To control the Majlis, the Shah used the gendarmerie and local police to supervise parliamentary elections to his satisfaction. In addition, services formerly provided to the peasants by the landowners, such as fertilizer, seed, finance, and the like, were assumed by the government, bringing the peasants under the dominance of the political center in Tehran.

Although much political thought was given to land reform, in terms of gaining the loyalty of the rural masses and circumscribing the power of large landowners, scant consideration was given to improving the performance of the agricultural sector. Although land reform gave some farmers the opportunity to enter the modern economic sector, it was generally ill-conceived. There was no significant redistribution of wealth; rather, the bulk of agricultural land was parceled into uneconomic holdings. Land reform ignored the problems of the poorest members of the rural community, the large group of landless laborers (approximately 25 percent of the work force). Another complaint was that land reform was late in coming (2 million persons fled the countryside between 1956 and 1966). The major criticism of land reform was that it failed to deal with the key issue of increased productivity. Prior to the early 1960s, Iran was largely self-sufficient in food production; but with increased industrialization, the country became dependent upon foreign imports. Overall, the government lacked administrative ability or will to conduct the tedious and unglamorous business of land reform; "the introduction of land reform coincided with the beginning of a sharp decline in agriculture's overall importance in the economy. Some claim that the Shah deliberately sacrificed agriculture in order to concentrate on building up an industrial base."[17]

In addition to strengthening the loyalty of the peasants on the side of the Shah to counteract the perceived threat posed by the rising professional middle class, the White Revolution—and land reform in particular—represented an attempt to preserve traditional power relationships, specifically control from above. The tentacles of central government and increased control stretched to all corners of Iranian society.

THE ECONOMY AND POLITICAL CONTROL

The acquisition of absolute power in the eyes of the Shah required pervasive involvement in the national economy. This was possible due to the ever-increasing oil revenue of the 1960s and the oil price hike that occurred in 1973. Prior to his deposition, wealth cemented the government of Mohammad Reza Pahlavi.

The Shah was involved in all aspects of the national economy, serving in one capacity or another as operator and regulator over the state economic structure. Whereas Reza Shah had amassed a private fortune to ensure control, his son was adept at obfuscating the distinction between state funds and royal funds, making both accessible to himself. The Shah's economic power was especially important in terms of his control over the oil industry and the revenue derived from it. The chairman of the National Iranian Oil Company was appointed by and answerable only to the Shah. It is believed that the NIOC was used as a source of supplementary funds for the regime to sustain monarchical power. Another economic resource was the Pahlavi Foundation, ostensibly a charity organization established and financed from the Shah's own wealth. The foundation served a myriad of purposes; essentially it was used as a way to exert economic control or influence through investment in specific sectors of the economy, as a source of funds for royal ventures, and as an institutionalized conduit for "pensions."[18] An editorial that appeared in a leading publication (1965) summed up the extent to which the Shah's government was involved in the economic structure of Iranian society:

> . . . in this economy, all roads lead to the State. The State produces textiles, shoes, canned fruit, chairs, desks, wire, and even poultry. The State is a businessman, dealing in sugar, paper, automobiles, oil, typewriters, and even cosmetics. The State is a farmer and a fisher; the State is a dairyman selling milk and eggs; the Government breeds cattle, it operates bakers and groceries.
>
> When we talk of the Government, we do not refer to the Cabinet, but to the Administration. They oppose the transfer of the State monopolies to the people. It obstructs this as long as it can and then it spoils the whole thing. . . .[19]

Foreign capital and investment flowed into Iran in late 1973, resulting in rapid construction of modern enterprises. Foreign imports increased, especially consumer goods, catering largely to Tehran's middle and upper classes. Those who suffered most from the Shah's economic policies were the traditional merchants, artisans, and moneylenders. Smaller, locally run enterprises faced government-sponsored domestic as well as foreign competition, the unavailability of credit, and government restrictions that hampered operations. The government moved toward greater control of trade and a weakening of the bazaars.[20]

Even in agriculture, the major portion of government investment went into large productive units, farm corporations, and agribusiness, resulting in the displacement of large numbers of peasants who were forced to seek employment in towns and cities. Iran, once largely independent in food production, became dependent upon food imports (wheat from Oregon, rice from New Orleans, oranges from Israel, etc.). The influx of foreign investment and foreign imports (food, goods, and services) transformed Iran into a dependent consumer nation. The fact that the Shah allied himself with foreign investment and capital at the expense of indigenous economic development engulfed the country in consumerism and dependence on foreign economic resources. Economic dependence on the regime made for greater control by the political authority, expanding the autocratic power base of the Shah.

The sweeping intervention of the political authority in the economic structure of Iranian society was a method of legitimization and system preservation for the regime. Independent businesses were anomalous in this economic structure. In one form or another, the government had a hand in the economic life of the country.

The White Revolution was intended to promulgate the image of a monarch who was all things to all people, regardless of social gradation, thereby providing his regime approval and legitimacy. When control through political and economic means failed, the Shah did not hesitate to resort to the prodigious coercive power at his disposal (prison, torture, exile), calling upon the vast security and secret police network fashioned during his regime.

PAHLAVI POLITICS: THE MAINTENANCE OF POWER

The words of Niccolò Machiavelli regarding the relationship of ruler to ruled in terms of the maintenance of power in the sixteenth century are commensurate with the political thinking and style of Mohammad Reza Pahlavi in the twentieth century: "For it may be said of men in general that they are ungrateful, voluble, dissemblers, anxious to avoid danger, and covetous of gain; as long as you benefit them, they are entirely yours; they offer you their blood, their goods, their life and their children. . . ."[21]

The traumatic events of 1953 in which the authority of the Shah and the traditional patterns of government were severely shaken gave impetus to the politics of survival that became the hallmark of his regime. It was noted that the Shah "deliberately fragmented and weakened the authority of all individuals and institutions that might challenge him. His own power has been buttressed by repression and a refined system of rewards."[22]

Governmental administration in Iran was not based on the ideal of public service. Instead it was a system in which individuals served the central authority (the Shah), then particular individuals or interests, in that order. Survival politics was the norm not only of the Shah but of all those who surrounded him, whose power or position depended on proficiency in this area. The ability to maneuver and accommodate to the exigencies of Iranian politics, Pahlavi style, was a requisite to the maintenance of position and power. Members of the political elite could never be certain of their positions in the political structure.

The system of central, arbitrary authority was incongruent with the acceptance of responsibility and initiative, breeding instead ineffectiveness and mistrust. With decisions made at the top, removed from the source of the problem, delays and inefficiency reigned supreme. The political drama staged by the Shah was one in which the inherent divisions in society were used to political advantage. Distrust, lack of confidence in others, and personal insecurity endemic in Iranian society were reinforced by the political apparatus. The Shah's policy of divide and rule was remiss in evolving a sense of integration and identification among members of the political bureaucracy—a tacit political device. Cooperation essential to social action was absent in the governmental administration, stemming from the Shah's covert encouragement of the isolation and insecurity of individuals in his political structure. In a political system where isolation, insecurity, skepticism, and rivalry abounded, authoritarian leadership would appear more efficacious in terms of sociopolitical action. The Shah could more easily justify his absolute rule to the polity based on these divisions.

A cohesive bureaucracy and military was seen as a greater threat. With a large and unwieldy military and bureaucratic structure, the Shah minimized the chance of dissidence. The larger the institution(s), the greater the fragmentation, and, consequently, the less possibility for the development of effective power bases of opposition.

For the Shah's program of modernization to be effective, an administrative system was needed in which individuals would be willing to assume responsibility and initiative and in which authority could be delegated. The autocratic political structure of the Pahlavi regime could not risk delegation of authority or the development of an independent bureaucracy. Authority patterns in Iran were not conducive to effective administration. Authority was often the only criterion for decision making. Individuals were hesitant to accept responsibility unless vested with authority; and authority was rarely delegated to those at lower levels, mitigating against the development of initiative. Communication in the political structure was primarily vertical, stifling cooperation and communication between co-workers and preventing effective functioning of the organization. Action had to be cleared with the main authority, the individual at the top. Nothing was to detract from the authority of the Shah. He perpetuated the image of a strong leader, seemingly aware of the political legitimacy attached to individuals who performed this role well.

The Shah's brand of administration was based on traditional patterns of personalism and informality. Most notable was the absence of effective institutions and agencies with clearly defined principles and goals and administrators with credentials commensurate with position. His government reflected the pervasiveness of *parti* (pull, or personal ties and contacts), tension, and competition. Regardless of the outward development of an expanded and formal bureaucracy, the business of ruling and decision making rested in personal networks. In order to achieve certain ends, individuals often found it easier to resort to personal contacts. Success and survival in the political system rested upon the ability to make the right connections and to have an intricate network of personal relationships.

The Shah's dominance of the Iranian political system stemmed from the support of foreign governments (especially the United States), an extensive secret police and well-equipped armed forces for internal control, rigid control over the freedom and civil liberties of the populace, and a subservient political elite. But in terms of the political culture of Iranian society, his prolonged success in controlling the political apparatus was based, it seems, on a keen awareness of the values and behavior of the polity in general and the political elite in particular. In a social system where rivalry and distrust in interpersonal, intergroup, and interclass relations has been pervasive, the Shah was especially adept at using these forces to his political advantage. The creation of overlapping positions and agencies, the arbitrary shifting of administrators and dismissals, and favoritism all aided in preservation of the existing ruler-subject political system.

This reliance on central authority, or rule from above, was reinforced through the Shah's modernization program. Legitimacy for the regime was derived from the government's ability to satisfy the material and power needs of the polity. By co-opting dissident elements into the bureaucracy, he preserved ongoing political patterns. Control over the economic structure of society as well as the political apparatus provided the mechanism to meet the demands on the political system while at the same time controlling the nature of those demands. Modernization without commensurate sociopolitical development connotes reliance upon traditional political methods; in prerevolutionary Iran, this meant strengthening the authoritarian, personal rule of the Shah.

Power sustained by satisfaction of material needs, manipulation, and coercion would not maintain the authority of Mohammad Reza Pahlavi over time. Accommodation rather than national acceptance of the regime proved a shaky foundation for sustained leadership. For all his modernization efforts, the monarch was ineffective in gaining national legitimacy, particularly among the religious community, the traditional economic sector, and the growing professional middle class. Dramatic advances in industry and in the economy merely increased the populace's needs, especially for political participation and social justice. The Pahlavi regime encouraged rapid change but failed to develop the ability to absorb it. As sociopolitical demands heightened, the regime resorted to traditional patterns of authority and coercion. Political development was not a part of the Shah's modernization plan. Traditional power and authority structures were not altered, but bolstered.

Beginning in 1973, with the exception of agriculture, Iran experienced a period of dynamic growth based on increased oil revenues that year. With the rise in prices, Iran's oil revenues jumped from $5 billion to $19 billion or $7.00 per barrel over the previous $1.95 a barrel. Increased oil revenue created a euphoria within the regime, leading to a governmental policy of accelerated economic development. Despite exhortations concerning inflation, growth continued unrestrained, with the economy out of control by early 1975; land prices increased, as did wages and prices. Dependence upon imports and decreased agricultural production led to frequent scarcity of some basic items and a rise in prices, particularly of foodstuffs. The political authority was ill-equipped to deal with the rapid economic growth to which it had committed itself earlier. Many problems plagued the government during this period of new finance. Poor budgetary planning and discipline, infighting between various departments and ministries for the new income, inaccurate estimates of need, a shortage of manpower, ports unable to handle the overflow of imports flooding the country, and a generally inadequate infrastructure were just some of the problems the government confronted. Expenditures soon outstripped revenue; by 1976, the Shah had reversed his earlier bullish policy of economic expansion. Whereas in 1974 the Shah boldly announced that the Iranian people could expect more—for example, lower taxes, welfare—by 1976, the tone was markedly different. His tempered message to the people called for restraint; they were to work harder, to increase production, and to expect higher taxes, all for the good of the nation.[23] The Shah's advocacy of the idea of government capable of satisfying all the needs of the people was a dangerous precedent for a regime sorely lacking in national legitimacy.

By 1976, the polity had come to expect certain outputs from the government in Tehran—they had formulated beliefs as to what government would and should do for them. This sudden shift from abundance to belt-tightening had serious repercussions within Iranian society, from which the Shah never recovered.

The gap between what the Iranian people demanded and what they got from government increased, as did societal tension. Land reform, meant to win the loyalty of the peasants and co-opt them into the political system, created a climate of rising expectations among this class. One of the consequences of land reform and modernization, in general, was an influx of peasants to the cities, building tensions in the countryside, partly due to the breakup of numerous families, an important cultural stronghold in Iranian society. Villagers who were led to expect new conditions found only that the traditional landlord was replaced by impersonal government agents and that reform had altered methods somewhat but had not improved their lives substantially. The insecurity and inefficiency felt in rural Iran were also evident among the burgeoning bureaucratic middle class. Although brought into the political apparatus because of material satisfactions and position, the professional middle class was uncommitted to the political system. The Shah's emphasis on "revolution" was an admission of a fundamental need for change. The consequence of speaking revolutionary language, while preserving and acting in terms of old patterns, was widespread alienation of the professional middle class. The Shah found himself resorting more and more to physical coercion to maintain power. The anxiety and anger of the people became focused on the Shah, who, through his own machinations, perpetuated his image as ultimate decisionmaker and initiator of governmental policy. The frustration accompanying his modernization policies was felt by all strata of society, who in one form or another experienced the heavy hand of government.

The Shah and his political elite faced one of the fundamental difficulties affecting a traditional political system bent on modernization while clinging to old political patterns—the widening chasm between demands for greater political participation and social justice and the reluctance of the political authority to share power and satisfy demands. But as Bill and Leiden observe: "This situation is sometimes partially mellowed by the greater capacity to satisfy material demands that are also vital to the population. In this area, modernization plays a temporary, stabilizing role. In the long run, there must be an enduring capacity to satisfy continually and effectively the social and political need emanating from all groups and classes in the society."[24] In terms of its relations with the people of the cities and towns of Iran, the central government in Tehran assumed the role of "colonizer," extracting both human and economic resources. The center, Tehran, grew at the expense of the periphery as political control was extended over the countryside.

By the late 1970s, the ailing Shah found he could no longer control the sociopolitical milieu of Iran. The dissatisfaction of all groups and classes reached its apogee as the monarch strained to preserve the power structure he had constructed. Built on co-optation, balanced conflict, and imported modernization, it proved to be tenuous and unsustaining; even the United States proved to be an unreliable ally. Ironically, it was the traditional elements of Iranian society—the religious order—that secured the political legitimacy necessary to challenge the monolithic political, economic, and military structure ruled by the last of the Pahlavi dynasty.[25]

Although monarchs in Iran have had ultimate authority for centuries, in recent times the individual holding that office has had to work harder at keeping it than his predecessors did. Mohammad Reza Pahlavi's machinations and maneuverings to preserve power gave the picture of a monarch cognizant of the tenuous nature of his position. Not allowed active participation in the decision-making apparatus of the political system, the polity exerted a check on political authority through its oblique mistrust of those in power.

The uprising of the polity against the inexorable control of the Shah demonstrated the unique independence of the Iranian people. Although the monarch did everything in his power, as we have seen, to minimize opposition to his regime, his control could not reach into the traditional independent network developed over the centuries—the mosque as the purveyor of political opposition. It is interesting to note that during the Islamic Revolution, insurrectionary tape recordings were widely distributed in Iran through a network that ran from village to city. No amount of control from above could contain the influence of the opposition in expressing dissatisfaction with the political policies of the Shah. The political milieu and structure of the Pahlavi regime and overt influx of foreign capital and influence in Iran created an environment for dramatic revolutionary change. The concluding chapter examines in more detail the deposition of the Shah, the Islamic Revolution, and the foundation of the Islamic Republic.

VI

Islamic Revolution and Republic

The influence of the West altered the ancient monarchical system of Iran. For centuries the ruling dynasty appeared to base its power not on a standing army or an extensive bureaucracy, but on the disposition of the citizenry to submit to authority. The Qajar dynasty's collaboration with and concessions to imperial powers, military defeats, and the demise of indigenous industry due to the infusion of foreign competition introduced a crisis of confidence in which the monarch no longer wore the mantle of guardian of Iranian interests and independence. The loss of independence and prestige was intolerable in terms of Iranian political culture.

The disintegration of the monarchy began in the twentieth century, as the king of a dying dynasty reluctantly acceded to the demands of the polity for a constitution. This started a process of sporadic parliamentarianism from which there was no turning back. A new breed of middle-class professionals, intelligentsia, merchants, and ulama forced the legal end of monarchical absolutism in Iranian government. This evolutionary process continued until the 1970s, when the monarchical institution met its final end, as the political system constructed by Mohammad Reza Pahlavi crumbled around him.

Revolution does not merely occur; its seeds are sown in the past. The Revolution of 1978–79 was the completion of the Constitutional Revolution of 1905–9, and it was a self-liberating act to overcome the inferior mentality that went with domination by a repressive regime and an intrusive superpower.

EVOLUTION: CONSTITUTIONAL REVOLUTION TO MONARCHICAL DEPOSITION

A pivotal point in Iranian history is the introduction of constitutionalism in 1906. During this period, the state became an entity somewhat distinct from the person of the ruler; and the institution of the monarchy, at the heart of Iranian tradition for centuries, was challenged. The monarchical institution was confronted again in the 1950s with the emergence of a strong leader, Dr. Mohammad Mossadegh, who appealed to the cultural nationalism of the polity. In 1953–54, with the aid of the United States, the monarchy was reestablished as the center of authority. As explained in the previous chapter, Mohammad Reza Pahlavi's position was tenuous and lacked legitimacy from the beginning.

The independence and xenophobia that were hallmarks of the constitutional period did not diminish, but rather gained momentum as Iran experienced the political hegemony of the Soviet Union and the West: Russian and British intervention during World War II, the postwar turmoil over oil, and the large-scale introduction of American cultural, political, and economic interests encouraged by the last of Iran's monarchs.

Comparative Analysis—Iran's Revolutions

There are certain similarities between the Constitutional Revolution and the Islamic Revolution. Both the Qajars and Mohammad Reza Pahlavi were perceived as negligent in preserving Iranian independence. In terms of political output, the leader was to guard Iranian sovereignty. Political authority traditionally remained with Iran's monarchs as long as they continued to protect the country's independence and national sovereignty. In each period the aim of the revolutionaries was to eliminate foreign influence and check the tyranny of the monarch and the court. The Constitutional Revolution, the National Front movement led by Dr. Mossadegh, and the Islamic Revolution all share a common characteristic—the alliance of Islamic protests with secular reform movements.

One discernible difference between the two revolutions, which affected their denouements, was that the Islamic Revolution was a unified national movement involving Iranians from all areas and walks of life, whereas the Constitutional Movement was essentially an urban campaign with leadership and support coming from specific groups in Tehran. As in the Constitutional Movement, the ulama, merchant class, and intellectuals spearheaded the Islamic Revolution. But the latter movement broadened its support to include peasants and workers— generally apolitical—who became a major force substantially affecting the politics of postrevolutionary Iran.

An aspect of the Islamic Revolution that differentiates it from the Constitutional Revolution was the presence of shifting population trends. For example, the professional middle class, an important force for change, increased by over 60 percent between 1956 and 1966.[1] In addition, the population of younger Iranians underwent transformation; those under fifteen years of age increased from 42 percent in 1956 to about 47 percent in 1972.[2] In an analysis of social backgrounds of several hundred active opponents of the late Shah's regime who were imprisoned or executed by the police between 1972 and 1976, it was learned that well over 90 percent were young men and women of the professional middle class.[3] The Islamic Revolution was brought about by cadres from the middle class and working class, but also by rural migrants driven to the cities by the Shah's "modernization" of agriculture program. These groups were an important force because of their demands and expectations of government, which included economic stability and a greater voice in the political system.

Both revolutions were unique in contemporary Middle East politics, particularly in that the military had little to do with them; when the military did become involved in the Islamic Revolution, it generally joined the forces of change against the established order. In fact, the noncommissioned officers and technicians, whose ranks had swelled due to the Shah's large purchases of sophisticated weapons, played an influential role in the defection of the armed forces. Unlike other revolutions, the revolutions of the early 1900s and late 1970s in Iran were not the monopoly of a small group of elites, but sprang with enormous power from the polity's dissatisfaction with the status quo and from the general perception of various sectors of society that their interests were secondary to those of the industrial world.

Like the Islamic Revolution, the Constitutional Revolution produced *anjoman*s (councils), which sprang up all over the country to carry out the work of the revolution.[4] Within Iran's Islamic government is a system of revolutionary *komiteh*s (committees), located throughout the country, working within localities to create a cohesive base of support. Revolutionary komitehs were organized out of mosques, with the exception of those in factories, oil fields, or other work sites. During the Islamic Revolution, people of localities and neighborhoods formed revolutionary committees to coordinate activities; these were not dissolved afterward.[5] During revolutionary periods in Iran, the crowd has played a vital role in bringing about change. The elements of mass demonstrations, strikes, and boycotts were paramount in halting the political authority in each epoch.

Many comparisons between the two revolutionary periods might be drawn, particularly Iranian solidarity in the face of foreign interference, a determination to preserve Iranian independence, and a distrust of foreign influence. It is important to note that the tradition of religious protest runs through the revolutionary movements of this century in Iran. Although the causes were political and economic, the polity found expression in religious symbols and religious protest. What distinguishes the movement of 1978–79 from the Constitutional Revolution and the National Front activities of the late 1940s and early 1950s is that it was fought completely in the Islamic idiom. In the words of one observer: "What produced the Islamic form of the revolution was not Islamic revivalism so much as repression of other modes of political discourse."[6] The polity was able to express political-economic dissatisfaction through religion, and it would seem to be an expression with political staying power.

Nationalism in Iran appears to be based on a strong sense of culture, especially religion. The composition of Iranian nationalism in the 1970s is the subject of the following section.

IRANIAN NATIONALISM IN THE 1970s

The very existence of the monarchy for 2,500 years led Mohammad Reza Pahlavi to express his belief that the monarchical institution was the pillar of Iran's national identity.[7]

In Iranian political culture the sustaining force seemed to be the idea of monarchy itself and the policy and charisma of the individual who held that office. Monarchs who effectively combined charismatic qualities with the idea of the office were heralded in poetic verse and grand tales of exploits. But with the influx of new ideas into Iranian society at the turn of the century, plus the onerous policy of the ruling dynasties, the idea of monarchy began to erode. Traditional Iranian distrust of foreigners grew in direct proportion to increased foreign presence in the country. The Iranian government's response to this foreign influx was to become an overriding principle of survival for the monarchical system.

A more accurate analysis might be that the monarchy was tolerated as long as it preserved the national independence and prestige of Iran, as well as the religious and cultural heritage of the country. Serious abuses of power by the ruling monarch generally went unchallenged by the polity if these criteria were met.

The exercise of power is a fragile element in the Iranian political system, as demonstrated by the overthrow of the seemingly unassailable Pahlavi regime after many years of rule. The personal nature of political power, centered in a leader supported by the U.S. government, was a tenuous base from which to build political legitimacy. Like that of his predecessors, Mohammad Reza Pahlavi's power rested upon force and traditional acceptance of kingship; eventually he relied strictly on the former. The authoritarian nature of Iranian politics under the late Shah did little to facilitate political development or the establishment of effective political organization in Iran.

Political Legitimacy

"A flood of money does not a Great Civilization build, nor even bring greater prosperity to the nation and its people. What it does do—and Iran is by no means the only example—is bring obscene wealth to a handful of parasites at the top of the economic pyramid, a host of new and insoluble problems for the nation, and more insecurity and misery for the people."[8] Economic prosperity does not bestow legitimacy on the political authority of a country. This was especially the case with the late Shah's regime, since the vast majority of the people did not reap the benefits promised by the government. Modernization that involved the wholesale importation of everything Western at the expense of Iranian culture and economy further damaged the Shah's precarious legitimacy. Changes in the physical environment brought about by modernization did not alter the basic political system. Social justice, equality, and political participation were suppressed issues; emphasis was on preserving ongoing political patterns propitious to the regime.

As noted, the monarchy was not a source of national unity. Instead, resistance to political authority was in some respects a civic virtue in Iran, the norm being to survive and outwit authority, with acclamation going to those who achieved this.

As seen earlier in this study, distrust of foreign interests and influence has been widespread in Iran and was a factor in building nationalist coalitions.[9] The traditional economic structure, industry (local bazaars), and value structure were losing ground to an imported and suspect socioeconomic system—that of the United States. Those persons who normally would have supported the government turned against it due to government exactions. The recession that followed a rising prosperity led the government to make demands not only on the lower classes but on leading sectors of society. This gave added weight to the moral force that denied the government legitimacy.

As shown in this study, national unity in Iran springs from a deeply rooted cultural foundation, a rich historical and literary past, and a pervasive religious consciousness. Through these channels Iranians could express independence and individualism and seek to regain control over the political system and restore shared values perceived as in the process of diminution. It is this sense of history and tradition that gives shape and strength to the cultural nationalism of Iran.

In the late 1970s, the reality culture of Iran (imposed Westernization) came into conflict with Iran's long-lived value culture. The conflict between these two poles lay in the fact that progress in the West was generated from within its own structure, while in the East, and Iran in particular, it was imposed from outside. Rather than continuing with an imported form of modernization, Iran's Islamic revolutionary action indicated the desire to produce its own mode of progress commensurate with its cultural values and norms. The Pahlavi government had no organic relationship to the infrastructure of Iranian society.

While imitating Western surfaces, Iranians lacked understanding of their substance. Ultimately, when the impetus for revolution gained momentum, the polity responded to the law of Islam rather than the law of the state. Although the causes of the Islamic Revolution were economic and political, as we shall see, the shape it took owed a great deal to the long tradition of religious protest.

Islamic Nationalism and the Islamic Revolution

The potency of the Islamic Revolution evolved from its Islamic character. The Revolution was infused with an ideological, moral spirit. Within the last century in Iran, religion expanded further as a forum for opinion making and political articulation incapable of being throttled by the Iranian state. The fact that religion, culture, and ethnic community were stronger bonds than the political bond smoothed the path for revolutionary fervor in Iran.[10] The ulama of Iran, unlike their counterparts in countries such as Egypt and Saudi Arabia, were generally kept out of the governmental process, which gave them a solid legitimacy with the masses. It was the religious leaders who spoke the language understood by the great majority of people, especially the lower classes.

Historically, Shi'ite Islam in Iran has a revolutionary, messianic, martyrlike, antiestablishment character. It is based on the idea of justice and equality, with leaders who have sacrificed their lives for these beliefs. The month of Muharram, which commemorates the time when Imam Hossein was slain at Karbala by Caliph Yazid, has important social and political implications for Iranian political culture. For Shi'ite Muslims, Hossein became the symbol and example of protest against tyranny and injustice. For years the feelings of despair and hope for deliverance have been expressed through religious dimensions; externally Muharram is a religious ceremony, but tacitly it has been a highly political event. During 1978–79, Muharram emphasis shifted from passive weeping for Hossein to active fighting for his ideals and for the overthrow of the archtyrant, Mohammad Reza Pahlavi. Iran's religious leaders called for protest marches instead of the traditional mourning processions. Also, religious holidays became times for major demonstrations. For years during Muharram the late Shah was identified in the rozeh'khani, with the evil Yazid; this continued after the Revolution. The religious leadership could call on the Karbala themes of the past to demonstrate the injustice taking place in contemporary Iranian society. These themes—the destruction of family, community, and government —could be effectively applied to contemporary Iranian society by the religious leaders. The Karbala metaphor was transformed from a merely personal event to a sociopolitical commitment by the masses, which gave strength to the Islamic Revolution.

As a minority religion, with nearly 700 years of persecution, Shi'ite Islam was especially suited for the role it was to play in twentieth-century Iranian politics. As one observer notes:

> They learned to survive underground and strike back whenever they could. They organized secret cells and an underground communications network . . . used the bazaar trade guilds as their economic base, and organized philosophical discussion groups along the trade routes, where they discussed politics as well. . . .
>
> Perhaps because of the ever-present tension, the believers have kept up the cells and societies they had in the days of persecution. There is a network of mullahs (lower clergy) in every village and town and city.[11]

This network was instrumental in spreading the revolutionary message of religious leader Ayatollah Khumayni and other ardent oppositionists to the Shah's regime. The Shi'ite ulama were a timely force in 1978–79 because they provided leadership, structure, and a mobilizing ideology.

Iranian adoption of the Shi'ite brand of Islam rather than the Sunnite (dominant in most Arab countries), when conquered by the Arabs circa A.D. 640, reflected the interrelationship between Shi'ism and national unity and national consciousness: ". . . even up to our day, Shi'ism, with its overtones and its aroma of opposition, of martyrdom, and of revolt, is matched quite well with the Persian character—a character formed in the course of a long history which is very different from the history of other peoples nearby."[12]

It was on the basis of Islam, during the 1978–79 revolutionary epoch, that the average Iranian was able to cooperate with fellow citizens. In a political system where the monarch demanded deference from all levels of society, the mujtahids, in their relationship as representatives and agents of the Hidden Imam, were an ubiquitous threat to the ruling monarch. At the pivotal point in Iran's history when revolt against the ruling regime was an unquestioned reality, the polity of Iran found solidarity in two specific areas; one, in religion, and two, in antipathy toward intrusive foreign powers. Islam served as a medium and rallying cry for the disinherited and dissatisfied of Iran, which encompassed Iranians from all strata of society.

It was apparent during the Islamic Revolution that divergent ethnic and political groups in Iran set aside their respective ideological differences and threw their support behind Ayatollah Khumayni, regarded as the symbolic leader of the Revolution. Secular opposition to the Shah's regime was not a new phenomenon in Iranian politics; rather it dated back to the days of Prime Minister Mossadegh. In addition to the Tudeh party, which operated underground for years, members of the National Front (although many were co-opted into the political bureaucracy) covertly retained allegiance to the ideas of Iranian nationalism. Various Nationalist Front organizations, though illegal, survived during the late Shah's regime.[13]

Iranian universities were centers of opposition to the regime; the reform trends of Islam, expressed by Dr. Ali Shari'ati, found powerful support there. It is not surprising that the Iranian people, especially the young, found inspiration for the Islamic Revolution in the ideas of Dr. Shari'ati (1933–76), teacher, scholar, writer, and theologian. Dr. Shari'ati's vision of a radical, socialist reformation of Iran galvanized the young people. He was a sociologist and student of history and philosophy, educated in Mashad and Paris. He formulated and presented a lucid and coherent Islamic world view and ideology of social, political, and economic change. He believed that national leadership should be held by enlightened laypeople, although he did not dismiss the role of religious leaders as spiritual guides. He analyzed contemporary Iranian society from the point of view of Islamic philosophy and culture, and his writings were studied throughout Iran.[14] His writings appealed not only to religious factions, who reacted to the irreligiosity of Iranian society, but to politically minded individuals whose basic goal was deposition of the Shah and political independence.[15] In his writings, Shari'ati used religion as an instrument to emphasize the cultural identity of the Iranian people and to strengthen national consciousness in order to confront what he regarded as the cultural imperialism of the West and the oppression imposed by the Westernized Pahlavi ruling elite. As one observer explains: "Shariati's aim was to emphasize the potentially radical notions inherent in some basic Shiite concepts. He displayed in radical fashion the central emphasis in the dogma, shifting it from religion to the moral and political aspects of life in society. Shiism could thus be absorbed into the mainstream of Iranian political revolutionary thought."[16]

During the Islamic Revolution, there seemed to be two Islams—the progressive Islam of Shari'ati and the more orthodox Islam, based on the idea of caliphate, messianism, and tradition. The fluid, unorthodox ideology of Islam expounded by Shariʿati appealed to those groups and individuals interested in an Iranian renaissance based on political and social justice. Shariʿati was successful in explaining Islam as a viable, revolutionary ideology. For the more traditional elements in Iranian society—the subproletariat of unemployed new urban migrants and petit bourgeoisie whose religious background was formed around the drama of Karbala—the charismatic, traditional message of Ayatollah Khumayni offered hope in a world of injustice and corruption. There was something in Islam for all believers during the Islamic Revolution.

Between 1971 and 1976, the Shah resorted to crushing military and police control to deflect intensified opposition to his regime. His policy gave birth to an extensive antigovernment terrorist movement and well-organized guerilla operations.[17] The Shah's repressive measures merely hardened the resolve of the opposition to abrogate his political authority.

As evidenced by the Constitutional Revolution and the National Front activities of the late 1940s and early 1950s, the alliance of secular and religious elements of society in protestations against the ruling elite was not anomalous. This alliance proved a more formidable force in 1978–79 because of the intense repression of other modes of political discourse. It was in the mosques that the message of revolution could be echoed with little governmental reprisal. The mosques were a vital means of communication to the Iranian masses, being largely beyond governmental control.

Iran's mujtahids have wielded tremendous spiritual as well as economic and political power in Iran. Although at times aligned with the ruling elite, they were often the nemesis of the political authority, particularly when they came under attack. The power of the mujtahids stemmed from a reputation with the masses rather than from an official post.

The structural violence of the Shah's regime made revolution inevitable. Individualism, a cultural norm paid deference in Iran, was permitted by the late Shah as long as it did not challenge his political-economic apparatus. Enforced conformity and repressed individualism created friction and seemingly caused latent anarchy in Iranian political culture.[18]

It is true that Iran historically averted domination by outside powers (and colonial status). Iran never gained the experience of having a palpable enemy, thereby failing to develop the feelings of national unification inspired by such enemy control—that is, not until the Islamic Revolution. Although the sense of participation fostered by a struggle for independence against a particular foreign power was missing in the past, it was replaced in the 1970s by the polity's rancor toward the Shah and his foreign supporters and perception of them as the enemy. The despotism of the Shah and his American political-economic backers became the rallying point for national aspirations. In this sense, the Islamic Revolution was an internal, anticolonial struggle in which all strata of Iranian society could unite.

"Unless power is justified by linking it to accepted values, the governed are less willing to obey and question the right of others to hold power."[19] This was particularly true for Iranians in the 1970s. Iranian identity is deeply rooted in an illustrious past and pride in cultural values and norms. But the future designed by the Shah, into which the people were being driven, was filled with imported norms and technologies that were regarded as undermining traditional Iranian identity and life. One example of this was the breakup of the family, a vital factor in Iranian culture for centuries. The regime's agricultural program had the effect of driving male members of the family into the cities to sustain the family economically. Also, the extended family was becoming more nuclear as young middle-class persons, imitating their Western counterparts, moved to other locations where employment was to be found in government or industry. In the past a young married couple remained in the home of the parents. This tradition changed with Western penetration into Iranian society.

As seen thus far, four main factors of the late Shah's regime generated strain on Iranian political culture, leading to his flight on 16 January 1979: (1) dissolution of Iranian religious and cultural values—cultural dislocation; (2) perceived loss of independence and resources due to the prodigious influence and capital of visible foreign powers linked closely with the regime; (3) economic dislocation and hardship; (4) political and social repression by a centralized tyranny.

It was religion that gave expression to political and economic dissatisfaction, and it was the religious leadership that filled the political vacuum. This was not aberrant in terms of Iranian political culture, since religion has always been a source of national identity and national expression, a channel for public protest, and a control mechanism over the enormous power of the state. Islam is a powerful force for change in Iran, because its social thought so lucidly recognizes *al-nas*, the people, as "the basis, the fundamental and conscious factor in determining history and society. . . ."[20] The nationalism evoked during the Islamic Revolution seemed to be based largely on a consciousness of cultural identity, rather than being steeped in political ideology. It was constructed on a faith in traditions of the past, not as practices and ideas to overcome, but as a source of new inspiration for the present and for Iran's future.

The Islamic Revolution in Iran graphically points up the role of culture in shaping the political milieu of a country. The deep-seated cultural variables of Islam, the strong sense of independence from and distrust of foreign powers and malignant authority and consciousness of history, were gradually to move the Iranian people to unprecedented alterations in the basic political structure.

ISLAMIC REVOLUTION AND POLITICAL CULTURE

The Islamic Revolution in Iran was unprecedented in terms of Third World revolutions. In the words of one observer:

> The uprising which started in January 1978 and ended on 11 February 1979 was by far the most massive, broad-based and sustained popular agitation in history. An estimated 20,000 demonstrators died in the year of protest, while the economic institutions and public services were virtually shut down. The movement was unparalleled for its nonviolent but militant character, and for its discipline in the face of government violence. As such, it will long be studied for its lessons in agitational politics and mass organisation.[21]

The cadres for the Islamic Revolution came from the urban-based middle class—the ulama, bazaar merchants, workers, intellectuals, and students. Rural migrants driven to the cities by the Shah's modernization of agriculture policy also swelled their ranks.

Conversely, in terms of revolutionary struggles, the Islamic Revolution in Iran was unconventional in that people from all walks of life participated not with arms but primarily with the force of an idea. The strategy of the Islamic Revolution was based upon traditional methods of strikes, mass demonstrations, protests, and the like. Strikes paralyzed railways, postal services, the national news agency, radio and television networks; most important, oil workers of Abadan and Ahwaz went on strike. High schools and universities throughout the country were closed as students called for the end of the Shah's regime. Demonstrators destroyed banks and official buildings. The social and economic life of the country was paralyzed by the actions of the polity, thereby immobilizing the political system.

The issue of leadership also reflects the uniqueness of the Islamic Revolution. It began without a formalized leadership base; leadership sprang from the religious nature of the movement. Ayatollah Khumayni arose as the symbolic leader, catalyst, and guide. His role was not to decide tactical military strategy, but to inspire and unite the people through the power of words and ideas. The opposition seemed to have no organized, disciplined party or clear-cut program. Ayatollah Khumayni relied upon charisma and the rhetoric of Islam to pressure for his vision of an Islamic state, formed in the early 1970s.[22]

The Islamic Revolution in Iran might be described as an "internal revolution" of ideas and values, of consciousness, not only political but social. Commenting on Ayatollah Khumayni, Michael Fischer states, "For him the revolution was not merely a political or an economic one, but a moral one changing the tone and value orientation of the government and of social behavior."[23] Although the revolutionary goal was the overthrow of an autocratic, Western-leaning regime and all its trappings, the religious faction of the movement had other goals—the reinstitution of traditional cultural values based on orthodox Islamic tenets.

Iran's Islamic Revolution was indeed social as well as political, cogently demonstrating that the power of ideas was greater than the power of weapons. In addition to the unifying goal of ousting the Shah, the idea of a sociocultural revival gave force to Iran's Islamic Revolution.

The success of a revolution on the power of ideas without armed force reflects the political culture of Iran. As seen in chapter 4, Iranians have traditionally found cultural identity in literature and the spoken word. The articulation of revolutionary ideas mainly by Iran's religious leaders also reflects the close identification of religion and political culture. The themes of Iranian political culture analyzed in this study run through Iran's Islamic Revolution and events that followed.

POLITICAL LEGITIMACY AND THE ISLAMIC REPUBLIC

Authoritarianism, an important variable of Iranian political culture for centuries, was not abrogated by the Islamic Revolution. Because of his onerous policies and ties to the West, the Shah lost all authority with the Iranian people. After the Islamic Revolution, authority passed to a leader who was perceived as a firm protector of Iranian independence and integrity and a bulwark against social dissolution. Attachment to a strong, charismatic leader seems a distinctive feature of Shi'ite Islam and Iranian political culture. Ayatollah Khumayni was a likely candidate to become Iran's head of state, based on his widespread and proven legitimacy with the people. Since the Islamic Revolution, the political power and participation of the religious order have increased substantially, symbolized in the highest office of Vilayat-i faqih (Governance of the Islamic Jurisprudent), currently held by Ayatollah Khumayni. This office is the central institution in the state structure of the Islamic Republic. According to article 109 of the Constitution of the Islamic Republic of Iran, the leader who occupies the Vilayat-i faqih must demonstrate competence in theology and sufficient piety to deliver a formal opinion, the ability to attract followers, and sufficient political and social insight, courage, strength, and potential for leadership. The duties and powers of the Vilayat-i faqih, according to article 110, are to appoint the commanders-in-chief of the three armed forces, to declare war, to confirm the appointment of the president, to dismiss the president in concert with the Supreme Court, and to appoint six members of the clergy to a twelve-member Council of Guardians, which can veto Majlis legislation viewed as contrary to Islam and has the authority to select a successor or council of successors to the Vilayat-i faqih.[24]

On a purely secular level, Ayatollah Khumayni personified the approved Iranian leader—charismatic, aged, learned, honest, and a man of authority.[25] In a clerical sense he could be closely identified with traditional religious images. Like Ali, he combined religious and political leadership; like Hossein, he was perceived as preserving justice against all odds; and like the Imams, he had access to esoteric wisdom and power, yet eschewed materialism and hedonism. Ayatollah Khumayni cultivated a populist language of confrontation against foreign intrusion in Iranian affairs and against the rich and intellectuals. The interesting blend of secular political appeal and religious influences created a strong power base.

Ayatollah Khumayni's legitimacy as an opponent of the Pahlavi regime dates back to the 1940s.[26] In the 1950s, he welcomed the stance of Prime Minister Mossadegh against the oil colonialism of the West. In the 1960s, he openly confronted the government, condemning the Shah's violation of the constitution and the government's decision to grant immunity from Iranian law to American civilian and military advisers (and dependents) and leading a successful strike in 1962. Ayatollah Khumayni continued to preach to large crowds about their power to sweep away the Pahlavi regime. Exiled in 1964, he was unrelenting in his condemnation of and call for liberation from the injustice and corruption of the Pahlavi regime. Ayatollah Khumayni's strong antipathy toward all forms of foreign influence in Iran merely increased his legitimacy with the Iranian people. The following observation regarding kingship in Iran has application to the leadership of Ayatollah Khumayni in the Islamic Republic of Iran and also seems to express his authority in terms of Iranian political culture: "Iranian political development is not yet at the stage where loyalty of the people can be to the idea of state in the absence of a symbol in the person of the king."[27]

The transfer of power from a monarch to a religious leader has not altered its authoritarian nature. Although religion has provided legitimacy for the new leadership, it also presents some serious problems. At the core of Shi'ite doctrine is a basic distrust of all government. In the past, it was generally the rule of the ulama to stay outside of government, guiding political events externally. Although they actively opposed many regimes, they never pressed for ultimate political power for themselves. The religious order has created a precarious situation for itself by becoming the "political authority" and stepping inside the political system. The dangers of this position are best expressed in the following statement:

> The mullahs have always been the dissenters, the martyred ones struggling on behalf of the poor masses against the authorities. But now, in an Islamic Republic, the mullahs will have so implicated themselves with the Government that political opposition becomes anti-Islamic. The traditional channels for dissent have been eliminated.[28]

A question for the postrevolutionary government of Iran is who will fill the vacuum as the countervailing element in the political realm if the traditional channel of dissent is engaged in the day-to-day affairs of government. The power of the ulama throughout Iranian history as a check on the arbitrary power of the state is a vitally important factor in Iranian politics and an essential question for the political future of the Iranian state. The sporadic opposition of divergent groups, primarily of the Left, that has surfaced in postrevolutionary Iran does not have the organization, cooperation, or support and trust that have been the strengths of the religious opposition. By assuming political authority, the ulama may have forfeited their moral authority. The boundary between clerical claims to be the moral guides to society and direct involvement in daily politics was ambiguous until 1979.[29] The Islamic Republican party and Ayatollah Khumayni have arisen from the ashes of the Islamic Revolution as the new political elite, a religious elite; and the authoritarian patterns of the past persist.

Individualism and the Islamic Republic

The individualism that developed over time as a survival mechanism due to countless invasions and oppressive rule is an element of Iranian political culture that may prove an obstacle in the creation of political nationalism and political stability in postrevolutionary Iran. Although culturally united, Iranians have generally found little common ground politically. The Islamic Revolution provided political commonality centered in freedom from an unpopular regime and foreign domination. Once these unifying factors no longer existed, centrifugal forces emerged revealing divergent interests, aims, and political leanings within the population.

Under the authoritarian rule of Iran's monarchs, the individual was isolated and society was atomized, and these variables served Iran's monarchs well to further continued domination. By undermining trust among members of society, the elite could more easily manipulate society. The need for mutuality and community spirit to overcome the mistrust and individualism of Iranian culture was one of the themes of public lectures by the ulama in Tehran during the 1960s.[30] The lack of trust that seems to characterize Iranian political culture is a deleterious factor in Iran's postrevolutionary pursuit of political objectives. Association is based on trust, and the Iranians' inexperience in association will be one of the more difficult problems confronting the nascent Islamic government as it attempts to construct a viable state.

The development of a national political consciousness and an idea of citizenship are necessary to the creation of an effective state. Social change and development in postrevolutionary Iran will require that certain constraining cultural norms described herein be abandoned.

THE MODEL AND FORM OF THE ISLAMIC REPUBLIC OF IRAN

The Islamic Republic of Iran might be likened to Plato's *Republic*: government by the specially chosen and specially trained (in Iran, the religious order). It is interesting to note the choice of the word *Republic* to describe the new government of Iran. Ayatollah Khumayni's authoritative position as Vali-ye-faqih in the Islamic Republic might be likened to Plato's "philosopher-king"—an individual who, through the force of knowledge and wisdom, performs the function of ruler, controlling the affairs of state.[31] Ayatollah Khumayni has not compromised with forces opposing his view of Shi'ite Islam; he has not been above using tactics to pressure various elements to achieve critical objectives and to pursue his vision of a moral Islamic government and society.

This Platonic divergence has some interesting parallels in regard to the shaping of government in postrevolutionary Iran. Although Ayatollah Khumayni is recognized as the guiding force behind the Islamic Republic, much debate has raged over the extensive powers of the Vilayat-i faqih as outlined in the constitution. And based on the monarchical history of Iran, there is a tendency to feel some consternation as to the powers of this position in the future, trading a secular monarch for a religious one.

Plato recognized that the omission of law from the ideal state was a paramount handicap to the development of the state. People being what they are, the state based on law became Plato's second choice, although he never quite abjured his concept of the state under the guidance of a philosopher-king. Law is essential to the functioning of the Islamic Republic if it is to endure. For Ayatollah Khumayni, a student of Islamic jurisprudence, and his followers, the Quran has become the model for Iranian society. The relevance of laws to the functioning of a state must not be underestimated. This is especially so in Iran, where in the past the absence of enforced laws made individuals fall upon their own resources and seek security in isolation from the larger community. The arbitrary enforcement of Iranian laws under the shahs created a milieu of distrust, individualism, and often deceptive sociopolitical behavior.

If we look at the outward form of government since the Islamic Revolution, there are obvious parallels with the past. Although steeped in religious ideology, the political apparatus of the Islamic Republic reflects similarities to the governmental apparatus of the late Shah. Like the Pahlavi regime, the Islamic Republic has the overt appearance of constitutional government, with a parliament, constitution, and elected representatives. But the political apparatus of the Islamic government is also controlled and monitored by a central leadership, security forces, Islamic tribunals (military tribunals under the Shah), and a dominant party, the Islamic Republican party. Not unlike the Shah's regime, the Islamic Republic has developed an organizational framework, but this has not minimized the role of Ayatollah Khumayni as the final decision-maker. Although he tends to remain in the background, Khumayni has been pivotal in holding the government together in the divisive aftermath of the Revolution. The style has changed, but centralized control remains with one individual. The leadership of Ayatollah Khumayni is less obtrusive than that of the late Shah, but it is no less felt. As during the Pahlavi regime, the people play a passive role in decision making. During the Shah's regime, the rich were rewarded for their loyalty and the middle-class co-opted into government. In the Islamic Republic, the lower classes or *mostazʿefin* (disinherited/oppressed) are rallied in support of the government. The government, particularly Ayatollah Khumayni, has cultivated this group; he has in a sense co-opted their support as a counter to the forces of opposition. The end result, as during the Shah's regime, has been to mollify the opposition. The lack of predictability that characterized the Pahlavi regime also characterizes the Islamic Republic. Political action based on personal inclination rather than prescribed regulations and laws has produced arbitrary government, based on survivorship. Those involved in it become adept at political maneuvering. This was especially true during the late Shah's era and appears to be so in the Islamic Republic.

The Islamic Republic, like its predecessor, maintains authority at the top, a security system, and suppression of opposition. The political actors and ideology of government have changed, but the structure has not changed much. The authoritarian, elite, and nonparticipatory political culture continues. The efficacy of the Islamic Republic depends largely on its ability to meet the social, economic, and political needs of the people and also on how it reacts to the long-standing political culture of Iran.

CONCLUSION

The quintessence of the Islamic Revolution was the unity of the polity against the late Shah and his supporters. This deeply felt ideal made it possible for Iranians to rid themselves of a form of government 2,500 years in the making. But what of political culture in terms of the government that has taken shape?

The ultimate leadership that has developed (namely, Ayatollah Khumayni) shows remnants of traditional Iranian political culture—regard for strong authority and vociferous opposition to foreign interference in Iran. Although he has attempted to place himself above the daily political conflicts, he is the final arbiter in disputes. As defender of the nation, he continues to attack "satanic" outside forces: the United States, Israel, the Soviet Union, and Iraq.

The individualism that made survival and vitality possible under the arbitrary rule of the shahs must be engaged to affect parliamentary government in Iran if it is to work. Cooperation and coordination must be learned, with group action playing a more productive part in Iranian society. Land reform will not work if the peasants are unable to work with others. This aspect of Iranian political culture is of paramount importance to reconstruction of a viable political system. Ayatollah Khumayni has seemingly recognized that coordination is essential to the achievement of unity for the Muslim world: "The crux of all problems of Islamic countries is division of word and lack of coordination. The key to victory is unity of word and establishment of coordination. . . . Refrain from discord, separatism, and group loyalty which are the basis of all troubles and regressions."[32] If this is true of the entire Muslim world, it is particularly applicable to Iran's political development.

There are lessons to be learned from the failure of the late Shah's regime. In a country of diverse social groups and classes, he failed to open the political process, to broaden the social base, and to forge links between his regime and the new classes. Instead, he leaned on the power of the military, his security organization, patronage, and the bureaucracy to sustain his regime. The Islamic government of Iran has not opened the political process to various social classes and groups, but depends on a religious elite that fills positions within parliament, in the bureaucracy, and in the Pasdaran-e Engelab (Revolutionary Guard) and on the support of the lower classes, at the expense of others. The Revolutionary Guard was established by a decree issued by Ayatollah Khumayni, and a separate Ministry of Pasdaran was created. While the regular army remained in place, the Revolutionary Guard developed as a second army. Under the wing of the Islamic Republican party (IRP), the Revolutionary Guard has acted as a counterweight to both the regular army and the parties of the Left. Internally the Revolutionary Guard played a key role in suppressing the antigovernment movement after June 1981; externally it has participated in the war against Iraq. It can be viewed as the coercive and military arm of the revolutionary government.[33]

With the ouster of President Bani-Sadr, the middle class was essentially removed from political representation. Bani-Sadr was the product of a clerical home and secular education. A supporter of the National Front and active in oppositional politics while attending Tehran University in the early 1960s, Bani-Sadr remained active in opposition groups, committed to the overthrow of the Shah, while he continued his studies in Paris. He was drawn to Ayatollah Khumayni in 1962–63 when Khumayni began his campaign against the policies of the Shah. The two met in 1972, and Bani-Sadr soon became a disciple. Bani-Sadr flew back to Tehran in January 1979 with Khumayni; and shortly after the Revolution, he became a member of the Revolutionary Council. He briefly served as foreign minister, then minister of finance, and ultimately became the first president of the Islamic Republic in June 1980. Bani-Sadr played an important role in the decision to nationalize Iranian banks and major industries. As a member of the Assembly of Experts, he attempted, though unsuccessfully, to strengthen the constitutional guarantees for individual rights. Disagreements with Prime Minister Mohammad-Ali Raja'i (the Islamic Republican party candidate for the post of prime minister) over ministerial appointments, as well as challenges and conflicts with factions of the IRP over the structure and function of the revolutionary government and his role in it, led to the downfall of Bani-Sadr as president in June 1981.[34] With the removal of this buffer, clearer divisions were drawn between the religious Right and factions of the Left. The Islamic Republican party, through its policies and rhetoric, has divided rich and poor, educated and uneducated masses. Rather than building a national consciousness, the aim in post-revolutionary Iran seems to be the construction of an Islamic consciousness. In many ways the political process appears to be as closed as it was during the Pahlavi regime.

Although Iranians have displayed a dynamic cultural nationalism, especially in the last century, the nationalism necessary for political development has been conspicuously absent. The Islamic Revolution created a new sense in the Iranian people; it demonstrated their political effectiveness and created a psychological identification with the affairs of state. Although Iranians experienced a sense of pride through the Islamic Revolution, only with time and habit can a sense of identification, integration, and trust develop.

The government of Iran after the Revolution faces not restoration but restructuring. Political organization and the amalgamation of various political and ethnic groups into the political life of Iran are necessary for the viability of the new Iranian state. These goals are essential to replace the reliance on the emotional aspirations of the people, which gave inspiration and endurance to the Islamic Revolution.

With the tyranny of the monarchical system removed, a new rhetorical device was required. Islam in its original form effectively united for a period of time large numbers of diverse tribes, regions, and people. In the contemporary world, Islam has divided into factions and has lost its cohesiveness as a sustaining ideology. It was Ali Shari'ati who called for the rejection of thirteen centuries of corruption and a return to the original purity of Islam with social justice. Shari'ati was looking toward the consultative, more democratic Islam. This was the rhetoric that appealed to the young and secular groups who took up the banner of the Islamic Revolution; and it is they who must be incorporated into the nascent political system. The diversity of thinking about Islam during the Revolution has been circumscribed in the shaping of the Islamic Republic. For many Iranians, it is necessary to define Islam before making it the foundation of government. Although Ayatollah Khumayni has the support of the lower classes—workers' salaries have doubled since the Revolution and generous subsidies are granted to peasants—moderate nationalists with influence in areas such as education and the economy (who are often dubious of clerical power) must feel they have a role to play in the new government of Iran.

The religious core of the Revolution was not aberrant in terms of Iranian political culture. Political change in Iran in this century has found expression in religion. In societies such as Iran, religion not politics is a mass phenomenon; and it was through religion the masses were politicized. But if we look back at the Revolution of 1978–79, it becomes apparent that the Islam that sparked the Revolution had many faces: the Islam of Shari'ati evoking a sense of cultural renaissance; and the Islam of the caliphate with influence centered in the Imams and the ulama, a more traditional, orthodox ideology. Islam spoke to almost everyone during the Revolution, but its message was different among classes and individuals.

We have seen how the forces of political culture have influenced social action and the political process in Iran throughout the revolutionary period of the late 1970s. The antiauthoritarian and revolutionary political culture of Iran resisted the authoritarian political culture that existed for centuries. We have seen how the revolutionary political culture of

Iran, which resisted Arab, British, and Soviet influence in the past, rose up against the capricious rule of an illegitimate monarch and domination by the United States. As in the past, group action in the form of demonstrations, boycotts, and strikes was galvanized when economic and cultural interests and national integrity were threatened. But one of the prevailing problems that confronts the Islamic Republic of Iran is partially a result of the authoritarian political culture of the past, in which power was maintained by dividing individuals and groups from each other. The vast gap between mass culture, which is more traditional, and elite culture, which is acculturated to modern ways, makes it difficult to bring these divergent groups into harmony for the common good of the emerging Iranian state. Although cultural nationalism has traditionally characterized Iranian political culture, the Islamic Republic will require a shift toward political nationalism, in which all citizens feel a sense of participation in the governmental process. The key to Iran's political future is how to create an integrated nation-state from an unintegrated, amorphous society. In building an Islamic consciousness, as seen by the ulama, at the expense of a national consciousness, the Islamic government of Iran has deepened the gulf between social groups and classes. Islam is an important part of Iranian culture, but it is not the only component. As a political ideology it has yet to unite the whole polity. The issue of a cohesive nation-state rests in social reforms that will mitigate the differences between classes and groups and cultural reforms that will build public values, a national feeling to supplant regional and other local sentiments.

As we have seen throughout this book, the political culture of Iran was dominated for centuries by authoritarian rule from above. This long ruler-subject political culture makes more democratic government in this century difficult for a people unaccustomed to the habits required for such a process. Parliamentarianism or other democratic norms connote group participation and compromise. In the authoritarian political culture of Iran, decisions were made by the Shah and the ruling elite; political decisions and action did not include the polity. The people of Iran were acted upon; they were not the actors in the political drama. Considering the authoritarian heritage that existed for centuries and the attempts at parliamentarianism that evolved in this century, we can better understand the role of the person who occupies the office of Vilayat-i faqih. In a sense, Ayatollah Khumayni can be seen as a necessary link to the political culture of the past, while Iran experiments with a new brand of government. In the period of evolutionary transition to a more parliamentary government, devoid of monarchical authority, the personality and position of Ayatollah Khumayni may be a needed stabilizing factor. This link to a familiar form of political culture may be a necessary ingredient in order to give time for the development of the elements required for successful parliamentary government. Khumayni's dominant role is a reflection of the traditional political culture. If more democratic government has an opportunity to develop in Iran, links to the authoritarian political culture of the past should diminish.

Although there are many negative factors for the new Iranian political system, based on its long tradition of authoritarian political culture, there may also be some positive aspects for a government in the initial stages of development. For example, authoritarian norms might provide an important means of reducing strain on the new government, in that the polity is predisposed to accept decisions of legitimate authority; also, the demands on and expectations of the political system may be less. The nascent political structure in this postrevolutionary period reflects the authoritarian and antiauthoritarian political culture of Iran.

The revolution was not finished with the removal of the Shah. The Revolution of 1978–79 reflected the unity of the Iranian People, who had clear-cut goals, against a palpable enemy. The questions after the Revolution were how Iran was to be governed and what form the governmental process was to take; the goals and aspirations were not clearly defined. The second cycle of the Revolution evidenced the clash between Iran's authoritarian and antiauthoritarian political culture. Certain segments of the ulama with a fundamentalist and authoritarian bent were in direct conflict with the more moderate segments of the revolutionary coalition, whose antiauthoritarian nature tended more toward compromise with the economic, social, and political realities of postrevolutionary Iran. In its intractable attempts to monopolize political power, the fundamentalist branch of the clergy has alienated many of the more modernistic and relatively secular factions of Iranian society. Postrevolutionary politics in Iran exemplifies the struggle between mass political culture and elite political culture—the former struggling for superiority, the latter for political survival.

The enemy has been less visible during the second phase of Iran's Revolution because it is an internal enemy. Iranian political culture over the centuries has bred divisiveness, and political turmoil in postrevolutionary Iran reflected this fact. The unprecedented transition from a subject political culture to a more participant political culture will probably not occur quickly in Iran. New patterns of socialization will need to evolve to create a sense of political identity and civic responsibility and competence.

Since 1872, when a nationalist coalition opposed the Reuter concession giving Baron Julius de Reuter the banking and mining monopoly in Iran, the movement away from monarchical authority has evolved. The force of religion and historical roots of nationalism and dissent reached their zenith in 1978 as Iran moved into an entirely new political reality.

The political culture of Iran connotes a coherence and endurance in its political life. The durability of Iran's political culture is manifested in the ruler-subject, authority and elite form of government, plus the fragmentation between elite and mass culture that persists even though actors, events, and structures have changed. The cultural sentiments that condition the way the Iranian people deal with and manipulate power have outlasted shifts in power structures. The role of religion in Iranian political culture has reached a high point in the Islamic government of Iran. Although Iran has gone from monarchy to Islamic Republic, the strains of political culture remain intact.

Throughout Iran's history, the force of culture has moved and shaped political events. This book has attempted to show the constant, yet dynamic and evolving political culture of Iran.

Notes

CHAPTER I. INTRODUCTION

1. Verba, "Conclusion," 523.
2. Kluckhohn and Murray, "Personality Formation," 58.
3. Spiro, "Social Systems," 105.
4. White, *Science of Culture,* 167–89.
5. See Kroeber and Kluckhohn, *Culture.*
6. Almond, "Comparative Political Systems," 396.
7. Representative of the studies that stemmed from the issues and problems of World War II are Leites, *Study of Bolshevism,* and Adorno et al., *Authoritarian Personality.*
8. Beer and Ulam, *Patterns of Government.*
9. Almond and Verba, *Civic Culture.* The sociological concepts of Max Weber and Talcott Parsons provided the major analytic categories employed in this study.
10. Ibid., 32.
11. Pye and Verba, *Political Culture.*
12. Pye, "Introduction," 6.
13. Almond and Verba, *Civic Culture Revisited.*
14. Ibid., 397.
15. Pye, "Introduction," 8.
16. Verba, "Conclusion," 513.
17. Pye, "Culture and Political Science," 296.
18. Brown and Gray, *Political Culture,* 270.
19. Ibid., 271.
20. Pye, *Politics,* 145–46.
21. It should be noted that these are not the only aspects of Iranian political culture. There are various strands of political culture that run through the sociopolitical structure of Iran, and no single political culture has been clearly established.
22. Pye, *Politics,* 121.

CHAPTER II. THE LEGACY OF AUTHORITY IN IRAN

1. Following are some of the concessions granted by the Qajar monarchs: 1864—telegraph concession, British; 1874—right to build a railroad from frontier to Tabriz, Russian; 1876—fishery monopoly on southern coast of the Caspian, Russian; 1881—Azerbaijan highway concession, Russian; 1889—Imperial Bank of Persia (with right to issue notes, mining privileges), British; 1891—bank concession, Russian; 1893, 1898, 1899—highways and mining, Russian; 1901—oil concession throughout Iran, except five northern provinces reserved for Russia, British. Concerning the economics of this era, see Issawi, *Economic History*, 358–61.

2. The Treaty of Gulistan gave Russia possession of most of Transcaucasus; the Treaty of Turkomanchai gave Russia two Persian districts and a large indemnity and reserved military navigation on the Caspian to Russian ships. In a later annex to this treaty, Russia exacted from Iran special economic and tariff rights. For the text of these two treaties, see *Majmoo-ah-yeh Ah'd Nāmah-haye Tarīkhee-a Iran*, 127–34.

3. For more on this concession and the period, see Keddie, *Religion and Rebellion*, and Browne, *Persian Constitutional Movement*, 12.

4. Abrahamian, "Crowd," 184.

5. The Constitutional Movement is dealt with well in Abrahamian, *Iran*, 86–101.

6. Bast is a historical tradition of asylum. By seeking bast, one was free from official molestation and had the right, theoretically, of direct appeal to the Shah to hear the case. Bast originated from the practice of throwing oneself on the mercy of the Shah by seizing the stirrups or bridle of his horse. Mosques, shrines, and palaces were considered free from official disturbance. Telegraph offices were later added as places of bast, based on the popular belief that the wires ended at the foot of the throne.

7. The Iranian constitution consisted of two documents: the Fundamental Laws, 30 December 1906, and the Supplementary Fundamental Laws, 8 October 1907. See Peaslee, *Constitutions*, 2:396–411.

8. Abrahamian, *Iran*, 86; Arasteh, *Man and Society*, 102.

9. Additional analysis of the Constitutional Movement can be found in Kasravi, *Tarikh-i Mashruteh-i Iran*, and Adamiyat, *Fekr-i Azad-i va Moqadimeh-i Nahzat-i Mashrutiyat-i Iran*.

10. Bayne, *Four Ways*, 275.

11. The text of the 1907 convention between Great Britain and Russia is printed in Great Britain, Foreign Office, *British and Foreign State Papers*, vol. C, 555.

12. The Russians, who opposed the constitutional government in Tehran, supported Mohammad Ali Shah's attacks on the Majlis (the Shah controlled the Russian-officered Persian Cossacks). The first, in 1907, failed; the second, in 1908, was successful only in Tehran. In Tabriz the people fought bravely and defeated the Shah's forces there. Their resistance to numerous government attacks sparked constitutionalists in other areas. Tabriz was ultimately occupied by the Russians. In 1909, the city of Rasht sent a small army to capture the capital; in Isfahan, Bakhtiari tribesmen joined the Rashtis. The constitutionalists successfully occupied Tehran, defeating the royalists and sending Mohammad Ali into exile in Russia after abdicating. Constitutional government was restored (see Abrahamian, *Iran*, 92–101).

13. Ramazani, *Foreign Policy*, 103. For a historical account of British/Russian rivalry in Iran, see Ullman, *Anglo-Soviet Relations*, 3:317–48.

14. A text of the Trotsky note is printed in Great Britain, War Office, *Daily Review*, series 5, no. 78, 748; see also Communications between Sir P. Cox (Tehran) and Earl Curzon, in Great Britain, *Documents*, 1st series, 4:1207–11.

15. Memorandum by Earl Curzon on the Persian Agreement, in Great Britain,

Documents, 1st series, 4:1119–22; and Memorandum on the Persian Question by Mr. Ovey, ibid., 13:541–45.

16. Ullman, *Anglo-Soviet Relations,* 383–89; Communications between Mr. Norman (Tehran) and Earl Curzon, Great Britain, *Documents,* 1st series, 13:729–32, 735–36; Keddie, "Iranian Power Structure," 2:10.

17. Haas, *Iran,* 217.

18. For more on Reza Shah's policy see Pfaff, "Disengagement from Traditionalism," 424–25.

19. Bill and Leiden, *Middle East,* 134.

20. Pfaff, "Disengagement," 425.

21. Bayne, *Four Ways,* 284.

22. Millspaugh, *Americans in Persia,* 35.

23. Bayne, *Four Ways,* 284.

24. For an account of this period see Saikal, *Rise and Fall,* 25, and Elwell-Sutton, *Persian Oil,* 105.

25. Kamshad, *Modern Persian Prose,* 85.

26. Binder, *Iran,* 65.

27. Lengyel, *Changing Middle East,* 306–7.

28. Kamshad, *Modern Persian Prose,* 86.

29. Cottam, "Political Party Development," 1:92.

30. For an analysis of the organization and political significance of the dowreh system see Miller, "Political Organization, Part I," 23:159–67, and "Part II," 23:346.

31. Cottam, "United States, Iran and the Cold War," 3:10.

32. At eighteen, Mossadegh took a government post in the province of Khorasan, serving for ten years. Upon his return to Tehran, Mossadegh joined in the revolutionary activities against the Shah's revocation of the new Iranian constitution. He then went to Paris, where he studied economics and political science for about three years; in 1914 he took his doctorate of law in Switzerland. Upon his return to Tehran, he wrote consistently in the Tehran press in favor of judicial and financial reforms. In 1915 he was elected to the Third Majlis; in 1917 he assumed the post of deputy to the minister of finance in the Nationalist government headed by the Bakhtiari leader Samsam al-Saltāneh. He was fired from this post for trying to dismiss a host of ineffective office-holders. When a pro-British cabinet succeeded in 1918, Mossadegh's outspoken criticism of the British forced him to seek refuge in Europe, where he remained until 1920. Upon his return, Mossadegh was appointed governor-general of the province of Fars, only to resign after the coup of 1921. Later he took the post of minister of finance (1922) in the cabinet of Qavam al-Saltāneh; this cabinet soon fell. He became minister of foreign affairs in Qavam's second cabinet, resigning the post on being elected to the Majlis. For Western perspectives on Mossadegh, consult "Iran: Expropriation," 35, "Iran: Dervish in Pin-Striped Suit," 29–35, and "Man of the Year," 18–21.

33. Cottam, *Nationalism,* 22.

34. Great Britain, *Correspondence,* 9–65.

35. Elwell-Sutton, *Persian Oil,* 188.

36. Ibid., 203. See also Dr. Mossadegh's statement of 30 Khordad 1330 (19 June 1951) in Fatih, *Panjah Sal-e Naft-e Iran,* 525–26.

37. "Iran: Expropriation," 35.

38. Elwell-Sutton, *Persian Oil,* 307.

39. Abrahamian, "Crowd," 190.

40. The issues and events surrounding the nationalization of Iranian oil are discussed in Keddie, *Roots of Revolution,* 132–41, and Alexander and Nanes, *United States and Iran,* 215–35.

41. Westwood, "Politics of Distrust," 358:128.

42. There are several accounts of CIA involvement in the overthrow of the Mossadegh government, among them, Roosevelt, *Countercoup* (Roosevelt was the CIA agent in charge of Operation Ajax); Harkness and Harkness, "Mysterious Doings," 34, 64–68; and Saikal, *Rise and Fall*, 44.

43. Westwood, "Politics of Distrust," 358:124.

44. Huntington, *Political Order*, 166.

45. Binder, *Iran*, 64.

46. Bill and Leiden, *Middle East*, 140.

47. Ferdowsi, venerable poet of Iran, completed his epic *Shahnameh* in the tenth century A.D. In some 120,000 verses, in which he attempted to use Persian rather than Arabic words as much as possible, he extolled the myth and history of Iran, singing the praises of legendary national heroes; see Shafaq, "Patriotic Poetry," 6:417.

CHAPTER III. RELIGION AND THE SPIRIT OF IRANIAN POLITICS

1. For further analysis of this idea, see Weber, *Protestant Ethic*.

2. Arasteh, *Rumi*, 6.

3. The Quran indicates that the message contained therein is a replication, confirmation, and supplement to previous revelations, especially the Torah of the Jews (Old Testament) and the New Testament of the Christians.

4. Nasr, *Ideals and Realities*, 96.

5. For an analysis of the political, economic, and social teachings of Islam, see ibid., 106–10.

6. The Iranian constitution of 1906–7 is translated in Peaslee, *Constitutions*, 2:393–411.

7. The Constitution of the Islamic Republic of Iran is translated by Dr. Changi Vafai in Blaustein and Flanz, *Constitutions*, 7:46.

8. By A.D. 732, the Muslim community extended from south France through Spain, North Africa, Egypt, Syria, the Arabian Peninsula, Iraq, parts of Anatolia, Iran, Afghanistan, and into Central Asia; a historical account of the development of Islam is presented in Zarrīnkub, *Bamdād-e Eslam*.

9. For a discussion of the state and law, see Hitti, *Islam*, 72–73.

10. Watt, *Islamic Political Thought*, 96.

11. Nasr, *Ideals and Realities*, 148.

12. Tabatabaʿi, *Shiʿite Islam*, 33–41.

13. After the deaths of Abu Bakr (first caliph) and Omar and Othman (second and third caliphs), Ali was elected caliph. He faced formidable rivals in Ayesha, wife of Mohammad, and Muʿāwiyah (then governor of Damascus). Muʿāwiyah (A.D. 661–81) established himself as caliph and began the Umayyad dynasty by nominating his son, Yazid, as his successor. Ultimately, family nomination became the norm for succession among orthodox Muslim states. Hassan, oldest son of Ali, was elected caliph by the people of Medina after Ali's assassination. Unable to conduct a civil war, Hassan temporarily agreed to abdicate to Muʿāwiyah, reserving succession to himself after Muʿāwiyah's death (he was much older than Hassan); these terms were amenable to Muʿāwiyah. But Hassan was poisoned through the machinations of Yazid. With time, the larger Islamic community came to acknowledge the line of Muʿāwiyah as the source of leadership. Much of the original spiritual orientation of the caliphate was lost under the Umayyads, and a form of kingship developed instead. For further analysis, see Rahman, *Islam*, 170–75, and Tabatabaʿi, *Shiʿite Islam*, 54–59.

14. The line from Hossein is said to have produced nine of the twelve Imams; four died of poisoning, whereas the others died in battle against the caliphs or were executed for sedition; see Farah, *Islam,* 177.

15. Cottam, *Nationalism,* 134.

16. Nasr, "Ithna Ashari Shi'ism," 100.

17. The relationship between the Safavid monarchs and the ulama is discussed in Akhavi, *Religion and Politics,* 13–14.

18. The reform movement of Zoroaster and the eventual creation of the purely Iranian religion of Zoroastrianism originated among a people who possessed a religion akin to that of the Vedas. The dates of Zoroaster's religious mission are nebulous (circa 660–583 B.C.), but it is known that in the fifth century B.C. his teachings became the official religion of the Persian empire. An interesting account of this religion is given in Jackson, *Zoroastrian Studies.*

19. Ibid., 173.

20. Karpat, *Political and Social Thought,* 377.

21. Zaehner, *Dawn and Twilight,* 298.

22. In addition to the revelation of Mohammad, Shi'ites attribute special revelations to Ali, as recorded in his personal copy of the Quran (the *Jafr*), passed from Imam to Imam.

23. Watt, *Islamic Political Thought,* 115.

24. The Safavids appointed religious judges and leading ulama to official positions; they sought and accepted advice and guidance of the most learned and respected men in the religious community. The Qajar monarchs continued to patronize and appeal to the religious authorities, but the penetration of Western influence mitigated the coalition between them; see Algar, *Religion and State,* and Akhavi, *Religion and Politics,* 10–15.

25. Bayne, *Persian Kingship,* 54–55.

26. Ibid., 44.

27. As an example, we see the long and rich history of Egypt and the apparent feeling that the pharaohs will never occupy the honored place for Egyptians that Iran's ancient rulers do for Iranians; see Frye, "Iran," 187.

28. Karpat, *Political and Social Thought,* 377.

29. Morier, *Adventures of Hajji Baba.*

30. Binder, *Iran,* 86.

31. The role of the ulama is described in Algar, *Religion and State,* 6–21.

32. Keddie, "Iranian Power Structure," 2:5.

33. Since Shi'ites believed tobacco that had passed through the hands of Christians was made impure, they were easily attracted to the movement opposing the granting of a tobacco concession to the British and faithfully obeyed the religious edict forbidding the use of tobacco.

34. Thaiss, "Religious Symbolism," 360.

35. Algar, "Oppositional Role," 232.

36. Jacobs, *Sociology of Development,* 223.

37. Browne, *Persian Revolution,* 19.

38. The vice-regent was usually the chief aid of the Shah, controlling all government departments. He was appointed by the Shah and usually was a man with little or no family background; the Shah regarded it as a threat to give this position to a person from the royal family or from the aristocracy.

39. Hairi, *Shi'ism and Constitutionalism,* 2.

40. Pfaff, "Disengagement," 421.

41. The effects of Western influence are discussed in al-Ahmad, *Gharbzadigi.*

42. Kashani was born into a clerical family in 1885. At fifteen, he went with his father to the holy city of Karbala in Iraq and lived there until both were involved in a religious war against the invading British in 1915. Kashani's political activity while in exile, during Reza Shah's reign, consisted of religious propaganda. He returned to Iran and political activism after the Shah's abdication. Unlike his fellows, Kashani was not wrapped up in moral and theological problems and was regarded by his peers as a political mullah.

43. On the Shah's land reform, see Hooglund, *Land and Revolution.*

44. Khumayni, *Islam and Revolution.*

45. Algar, "Oppositional Role," 246.

46. The text of the declaration given by Ayatollah Khumayni on 3 April 1963, commemorating the 22 March 1963 assault on the Faiziyeh Madrasa can be found in Khumayni, *Islam and Revolution,* 174–76; for more on the upheaval of this period, see Bakhash, *Reign of the Ayatollahs,* 28–30.

47. Lambton, "Reconsideration," 20:120.

48. *Kayhan,* 5 June 1963.

49. "Shah's Divided Land," 35.

50. Algar, "Oppositional Role," 255.

51. Godsell, " 'Rights' Critics," 3

52. Kluckhohn, "Myths and Rituals," 151.

53. Reza Shah forbade the excesses that marked these public ceremonies; for example, beating the chest with fists and chains, hitting the head with *qameh* (poniards), while chanting the name of Hossein. With Reza Shah's overthrow, these religious expressions resumed later in a more restrained manner. In former times, men dressed in white robes and marched through the streets; many would cut themselves, the blood staining their garments, to demonstrate their sharing of martyrdom with Imam Hossein. The ceremonies surrounding Muharram preoccupied a large majority of the population from all walks of life. On the tazia ceremony, see Chelkowski, *Ta'ziyeh.*

54. Thaiss, "Unity and Discord," 116.

55. Ibid., 116.

56. Upton, *History,* 111.

57. Thaiss, "Religious Symbolism," 359.

58. Gable, "Culture and Administration," 13:412.

59. Pfaff, "Disengagement," 426.

CHAPTER IV. SOCIOLOGICAL LINKAGES AND POLITICAL CULTURE

1. Parsons, *Structure and Process,* 175.

2. Schmitt, *Irony of Irish Democracy,* 2.

3. Nizam al-Mulk was prime minister under two Seljuq rulers. He instituted a series of schools in which liberal education was introduced at a time when religious teaching was the norm in the Muslim world. See al-Mulk, *Siyasat-nama or Siyar al-Muluk.*

4. Arasteh, *Man and Society,* 169.

5. Iranians are acutely aware of differences in social status, as reflected in the copious social appellations. Deference in behavior and speech is expected to be shown by a person of lower social position to those above and is granted freely. It is not uncommon to hear addresses such as "the Exalted Mr." or to hear a host greet guest(s) with a statement such as "our poor house and everything in it is yours, may we be your slaves." Letters end with phrases such as "sacrificingly yours."

6. Bill, *Politics,* 2.

7. The ultimate example of an individual rising in rank is Reza Shah, who came from a humble background through the military ranks to the very apex of power, establishing himself as ruler of the Pahlavi dynasty. "The ideology of upward mobility has made it possible for the ruler, in times of threat, to accede or grant power to non-elite, non-aristocratic elements. On numerous occasions, Iran has found the right man' who has led the nation out of what appeared at the time to be certain destruction or loss of identity" (Zonis, *Political Elite,* 126).

8. Morier, *Adventures of Hajji Baba.*

9. Zonis, *Political Elite,* 127.

10. Young, "Social Support," 6:126.

11. Several of Iran's most economically powerful men came from the ranks of the lower and bourgeois middle class. Others were former landlords who, because of the Shah's land reform program, tranferred their wealth to industry and commerce. The landless, rentier elite were those wealthy individuals who lost most of their land but refused to become part of the industrial elite, freezing much of their wealth in foreign banks; see Bill, *Politics of Iran,* 10–11.

12. Pranger, "Political and Economic Balance," 38:282.

13. Bill, "Social and Economic Foundations," 17:404.

14. Bill, "Modernization," 32:37.

15. Bill, *Politics,* 27. It is interesting to note that Mohammad Reza Pahlavi's second wife, Soraya, was a Bakhtiari; also, the prime minister (Bakhtiar) appointed in January 1979, in the midst of revolutionary turmoil, traces his heritage to this same tribe.

16. Kurds, Gilakis, Mazandaranis, Lurs, Bakhtiari, Baluchi, Qashqai, and Turkomans are just a few of the tribes in Iran; the Kurds form the largest tribal group. If a khan amassed a substantial amount of power, as did Agha Mohammad Khan, the first monarch of the Qajar dynasty, who gained control of fourteen tribal groups in other provinces, he became ruler of the nation; this was the course of events in Iran's long history.

17. An informative account of these oil negotiations is given by Elwell-Sutton, *Persian Oil,* 17–21.

18. For an analysis of the new middle class, see Bill, "Modernization," 32:26.

19. Behnam, "Population," 1:474–75.

20. An analysis of the political significance of the bazaar can be found in Miller, "Political Organization," 23:159–67.

21. Easton and Dennis, *Children,* 10.

22. Ibid., 11. An example of this independent learning through the socialization process is a child who has learned to dislike all authority figures, not because he has been taught to do so by his parents or because he is modeling the behavior of siblings or peers but rather as a result of what he interprets as unjust treatment by familial or other authority figures.

23. Esfandiary, *Day of Sacrifice.*

24. Frye, "Iran," 186.

25. McClelland, "National Character," 178.

26. Ibid. It is interesting to note that in his study of authority patterns in Iranian and Turkish societies through children's literature, McClelland found that in Turkey this same story took on quite a different interpretation. For Turkish children the story was morally instructive: individuals should not squabble, implying that authority is there to prevent such disputes.

27. For an interesting analysis of tarof, see Hillman, "Language," 337–40.

28. Bill, "Plasticity," 27:144.

29. Arasteh, *Man and Society,* 40.

30. McClelland, "National Character," 177.

31. Jacobs, *Sociology of Development,* 252.

32. For a more detailed analysis concerning Iranian familial relationships, see Davidian, "Application," 25:532–46, and Rudolph-Touba, *Marriage and the Family.*

33. Schmitt, *Irony of Irish Democracy,* 52.

34. Ibid., 55.

35. Bill and Leiden, *Middle East,* 71–72.

36. Esfandiary's novel centers around the multitudinous travails of one man as he attempts to replace a lost identity card, which requires that he involve himself with a web of government bureaucrats and an abstruse bureaucracy, which ultimately leads to his demise; see Esfandiary, *Identity Card.*

37. Rudolph-Touba, *Marriage and the Family,* 24.

38. Bill, *Politics,* 98.

39. This modern phenomenon is described by Van Nieuwenhuijze, *Sociology,* 393.

40. The precarious sociopolitical position of Iranian youth in prerevolutionary Iran is revealed in some unusual statistics: 75 percent of the suicides in Iran were committed by young people between ages fifteen and thirty; also, after the United States, Iran had the largest number of heroin addicts (with heroin the monopoly of young people); see Bill, *Politics,* 98.

41. Browne, *Year Amongst the Persians,* 133.

42. Arasteh, *Rumi,* 5.

43. The verses of this epic poem, completed circa A.D. 999, are still recited in the tongue in which they were originally composed. Modern Persian is nearer to the Persian of Ferdowsi than modern English is to the English of early writers such as Chaucer. The language has changed little during the last 1,000 or more years.

44. Wilber, *Contemporary Iran,* 35.

45. An example is the censorship of one of Iran's contemporary poets and literary critics, Reza Baraheni. Baraheni's translation of *Richard III* was barred from the stage when the minister of culture (the Shah's brother-in-law) saw it in rehearsal. It seems that the theme of Shakespeare's drama in which a king murdered his way to power was too close a parallel for the Shah's comfort.

46. Young, "Social Support," 6:129.

47. This was the accepted form of education for both upper- and middle-class urban youth. Occasionally a maktab open to all was established by a philanthropist. More often than not, the maktab was conducted on a personal basis between a family and the maktab-dar (instructor), who was generally a member of the ulama. The maktab system is described by Arasteh, *Education,* 6.

48. In 1926, there were approximately 2,402 maktabs with 45,998 pupils; by 1929, this number had been reduced to 1,890 with 35,931 pupils. See Sadiq, *Modern Persia,* 62.

49. *Ta'limat-i Dini Bara-yi Sal-i Panjum-i Dabistan va Sal-i Shishum-i Dabistan.*

50. Technical education was resisted in Iran, since the technical specialist was regarded as one who mastered only facts and therefore was not an educated man in the Iranian sense. The traditional disdain for manual labor and the lack of graduates with technical skills led to pressing manpower problems in Iran.

51. Concerning education during the period described, see U.S. Department of Health, Education and Welfare, *Education.*

52. Bill, *Politics,* 88.

53. Zonis, "Higher Education," 232.

54. Ibid., 233. In his study of political elites in Iran, Zonis recorded that 41.1 percent of the elite had university or postsecondary education; 50.7 percent had postgraduate education; 0 percent had no formal education at all; and 8.2 percent had secondary education only. In the general population, however, 67.6 percent of Iran's males had no formal education whatsoever.

55. Bill and Leiden, *Middle East,* 60–61.

56. Geertz, "In Search of North Africa," 16:20.

57. Pye, *Politics,* 41.

58. Bill, "Plasticity," 135.

CHAPTER V. AUTHORITY AND POWER: THE REIGN OF MOHAMMAD REZA PAHLAVI (1953–78)

1. Bill, *Politics,* 133.

2. For the Shah's policy of control, see Fatemi, "Leadership by Distrust," 36:48–62, Saikal, *Rise and Fall.*

3. Bill, "Iran and the Crisis," 57:328.

4. Graham, *Iran,* 130.

5. That patrimonialism in government breeds corruption was particularly evident in Iran. The dearth of official rules and regulations, loose organization, and personal authority patterns promoted a situation where individuals protected and enlarged their interests through various manipulative methods, such as bribery. Since personal political representation was nonexistent, individuals often resorted to other devices, some less than honest, to achieve goals.

6. Keddie, *Roots of Revolution,* 160–64.

7. Graham, *Iran,* 132.

8. Bill, "Plasticity," 27:150.

9. Zonis, *Political Elite,* 330.

10. James A. Bill arrived at this conclusion after two years of discussions and interviews with members of the professional middle class in Iran; see his article "Modernization," 32:37.

11. Bill, *Politics,* 54.

12. For more on this critical period, see Abrahamian, *Iran,* 421–24, and Keddie, *Roots of Revolution,* 150–56.

13. Jacobs, *Sociology of Development,* 182.

14. Ibid.

15. For a detailed account of the Shah's land reform program, see Hooglund, *Land and Revolution,* and Lambton, *Persian Land Reform.*

16. Zonis, "Political Elite," 28.

17. Graham, *Iran,* 43.

18. Pensions were synonymous with handouts or rewards for favors or fringe benefits to those faithful to the regime. The Pahlavi Foundation's interests in hotels, cement and sugar factories, the Iranian National Insurance Company, banks, merchant ships, and other industrial and commercial enterprises evidenced the extent to which the Shah and his immediate family were involved in the economic affairs of the country. An account of the Pahlavi Foundation is in Graham, *Iran,* 155–65.

19. B. Shari'at, "State or Free Enterprise." This editorial may have been written by the onetime minister of agriculture, B.F. Taleghani, also director of the B.F. Goodrich factory in Iran at that time.

20. Keddie, "Iran," 11:55.

21. Machiavelli, *Prince,* 61.
22. Graham, *Iran,* 206.
23. *Kayhan,* 26 October 1976.
24. Bill and Leiden, *Middle East,* 10.
25. America's role in the last days of the Shah can be found in Sick, *All Fall Down.*

CHAPTER VI. ISLAMIC REVOLUTION AND REPUBLIC

1. Looney, *Iran,* 118.
2. Ibid., 82.
3. Bill, "Iran and the Crisis," 57:334.
4. The anjomans of the postconstitutional period consisted of 6 to 100 members; some were religious groups and others conducted literary classes and emphasized education. Still others were terroristic, assassinating antirevolutionary leaders. Their activities were not directed by any central committee of the revolution. For more on anjomans, see Armajani, *Middle East,* 259.
5. For more regarding komitehs, see Azad, "Workers' and Peasants' Councils," 32:14–29; Bird, "Making Iran Safe," 559, and Siddique, "Islamic Iran," 6–7.
6. Fischer, *Iran,* 185.
7. Pahlavi Library Publications, *Bargozide-i az Neveshte-ha va Sokhanan-e Shah-an-Shah Aryamehr,* 35.
8. "Iran: New Crisis," 9.
9. Commenting on the atmosphere in Iran shortly after the Islamic Revolution, one Western writer notes, "Gone also—or at least diminishing—is the galloping xenophobia that used to be encountered everywhere" (Claiborne, "Many Iranians," A14).
10. A historical account of the Islamic Revolution can be found in Abrahamian, *Iran,* 496–529, and Keddie, *Roots of Revolution,* 239–58.
11. Armajani, "What the U.S. Needs to Know," 18.
12. Minorsky, "Iran," 201.
13. For an interpretation of the periods before and after the Islamic Revolution through the eyes of its former prime minister, see Bazargan, *Enghalab-e Iran dar Du Harakat.* Mehdi Bazargan was head of the provisional government of Iran from February to November 1979.
14. Following are just a few of Shari‘ati's works: *Tamaddon va Tajaddod, Ummat va Imamat,* and *On the Sociology of Islam.*
15. An analysis of the social theory of Ali Shari‘ati is given in Akhavi, "Shariati's Social Thought," 125–44.
16. Bayat, "Iran's Real Revolutionary Leader," 23.
17. A powerful military prosecutor was assassinated in 1971 after he sentenced thirteen young Iranians to death. Also, there was an attempted kidnapping and attack on the son of the Shah's twin sister in 1971. The deputy chief of police was assassinated in 1972. In 1973, an American military adviser was killed in Tehran; in May 1975, two U.S. Air Force colonels were assassinated; in 1976; three American employees of Rockwell International were killed in Tehran (see Bill, "Iran and the Crisis," 328–29).
18. Repressed individualism and its resultant anarchy seemed to be demonstrated in Iran's daily urban life; for example, the chaotic traffic situation in Tehran reflected the Iranians' disregard of policemen and traffic laws, which were constantly violated.
19. Shibutani and Kwan, *Ethnic Stratification,* 241.
20. Shari‘ati, *On the Sociology of Islam,* 49.
21. Ahmad, "Iranian Revolution," 21:6.

22. The beginnings of Khumayni's vision of an Islamic Republic are evident in Khumayni, *Hokumat-e Eslami*; recent publications appear under the title *Vilayat-i Faqih.*

23. Fischer, *Iran,* 216.

24. The constitution of the Islamic Republic of Iran (English translation) in Blaustein and Flanz, *Constitutions,* 7:52–53; for a good overview of the Iranian state structure of the Islamic Republic, see Benard and Khalilzad, *"Government of God,"* 119.

25. For a brief background description of Ayatollah Khumayni, see Bakhash, *Reign of the Ayatollahs,* 19–24.

26. In 1944, Ayatollah Khumayni was the only cleric who refused to rise when Mohammad Reza Pahlavi came to visit the Faiziyeh Madrasa, where Khumayni attracted large numbers of students with his discussions of political science from an Islamic point of view. In the early 1940s, he published a polemic that in part attacked the Pahlavi dynasty for its encroachments on the prerogatives of the ulama. See Khumayni, *Kashf al-Asrar;* also, excerpts from this book and other writings by Khumayni are in English in Khumayni, *Islam and Revolution.*

27. Bayne, *Persian Kingship,* 75.

28. Bird, "Making Iran Safe," 561.

29. A discussion of the political role of the ulama can be found in Bill, "Power and Religion," 36:31–41.

30. Akhavi, *Religion and Politics,* 119–20.

31. It is interesting that in his early days at the Faiziyeh Madrasa, Khumayni edified in the manner of Plato, with throngs coming to listen to the intellectual debate he inspired. His dialectic encompassed religion and politics.

32. From a speech delivered by Khumayni concerning the *Hajj* (Embassy of the Islamic Republic of Iran, 3–4).

33. A description of the Revolutionary Guard is found in Benard and Khalilzad, *"Government of God,"* 123.

34. For more on Bani-Sadr and his role in the Islamic Republic of Iran, see Bakhash, *Reign of the Ayatollahs,* 92–165.

Glossary

anjoman   Council; association

ayatollah   In Arabic: "sign of God"; high-ranking clergyman; an honorific title conferred by his followers upon a distinguished mujtahid

bast   Sanctuary from secular authority

caliph   Person holding the office of vice-regent

caliphate   Office of vice-regent after the death of the Prophet Mohammad

dowreh   Associations

fatwa   Religious opinion, decree, or ruling issued by one of the ulama, namely, a mujtahid

Hadith   The traditions concerning the sayings and deeds of the people

hajji   Title denoting the pilgrimage to Mecca

hijra   Emigration; Prophet Mohammad's emigration circa A.D. 632 from Mecca to Medina

Imam   In Ithna Ashari Shi'ism, one of twelve divinely inspired guides and leaders of the community who descended from the Prophet through Ali, the first Imam

Imamate   The institution of the rule by the Imams

jihad   Sacred war against the enemies of Islam

khan   A tribal chief; a title of respect

komiteh   A revolutionary committee within the Islamic government of Iran

madakhel   Perquisite; historical practice of selling official positions

madrasah   College or seminary of religious/Islamic learning

Mahdi   In Ithna Ashari Shiʿism, the last of the Twelve Imams, whose return will establish justice in the world

Majlis   Iranian parliament/National Assembly

maktab   Traditional elementary school, principally with a religious orientation

mostaz'efin   Disinherited and oppressed people

Muharram   First month of the Islamic lunar new year, which marks the beginning of a month of mourning for Imam Hossein

mujtahid   High-ranking clergyman who practices and interprets religious jurisprudence

mullah   A lower-ranking member of the clergy

al-nas   The people

pak   Clean, said of certain high-ranking ulama

rozeh'khani   Assemblies to eulogize the martyrs of Karbala

Sayyid   Descendant of the Prophet

Shariʿah   Islamic religious law

tazia   Dramatic performance, passion play, to commemorate the martyrdom of the Imams, especially that of Imam Hossein at Karbala

ulama (sing., alim)   Those men learned in the religious law of Islam

umma   The Islamic community

Vali al Allah   Vice-regent of God, said of Ali, the first of the Imams

Vali-ye-faqih   Individual who holds the office of Vilayat-i faqih

Vilayat-i faqih   The central institution in the state structure of Iran

waqf   Religious endowment

Bibliography

Abrahamian, Ervand. "The Causes of the Constitutional Revolution in Iran." *International Journal of Middle East Studies,* 10 (August 1979):381–414.
———. "The Crowd in Iranian Politics, 1905–1953." *Past and Present,* no. 41 (December 1968):184–210.
———. *Iran between Two Revolutions.* Princeton, NJ: Princeton University Press, 1982.
Adamiyat, Firaydun. *Fekr-i Azad-i va Moqadimeh-i Nahzat-i Mashrutiyat-i Iran* (The Concept of Freedom and the Beginnings of the Constitutional Movement in Iran). Tehran: Sukhan Press, 1340/1961.
———. *Fekr-i Demokrasi-yi Ijtema 'yi dar Nahzat-i Mashrutiyat-i Iran* (The Concept of Social Democracy in the Iranian Constitutional Movement). Tehran: Payam Press, 1354/1975.
Adorno, T.W., Elsa Frenkel-Brunswik, Nevitt Stanford, and Daniel Levinson. *The Authoritarian Personality.* New York: Harper and Row, 1950.
Ahmad, Eqbal. "The Iranian Revolution: A Landmark for the Future." *Race and Class* 21 (1979):3–11.
al-Ahmad, Jalāl. *Gharbzadigī* (Western Mania). Tehran: n.p., 1341/1962.
Akhavi, Shahrough. *Religion and Politics in Contemporary Iran: Clergy-State Relations in the Pahlavi Period.* Albany: State University of New York Press, 1980.
———. "Shariati's Social Thought." In *Religion and Politics in Iran: Shi'ism from Quietism to Revolution,* ed. Nikki R. Keddie, pp. 125–44. New Haven: Yale University Press, 1983.
Alexander, Yonah, and Allan Nanes, eds. *The United States and Iran: A Documentary History.* Frederick, MD: University Publications of America, 1980.
Algar, Hamid. "The Oppositional Role of the Ulama in Twentieth-Century Iran." In *Scholars, Saints and Sufis,* ed. Nikki R. Keddie, pp. 231–55. Berkeley: University of California Press, 1972.

_____. *Religion and State in Iran, 1785–1906*. Berkeley: University of California Press, 1969.

Almond, Gabriel. "Comparative Political Systems." *Journal of Politics* 18 (1956):391–409.

_____, and Sidney Verba. *The Civic Culture: Political Attitudes and Democracy in Five Nations*. Princeton, NJ: Princeton University Press, 1963.

_____, eds. *The Civic Culture Revisited*. Boston: Little, Brown, 1980.

Arasteh, A. Reza. *Education and Social Awakening in Iran, 1850–1960*. Leiden: E.J. Brill, 1962.

_____. *Faces of Persian Youth: A Sociological Study*. Leiden: E.J. Brill, 1970.

_____. *Man and Society in Iran*. Written in collaboration with Josephine Arasteh. Leiden: E.J. Brill, 1964.

_____. *Rumi the Persian: Rebirth in Creativity and Love*. Lahore, Pakistan: Ashraf Press, 1965.

Armajani, Yahya. *Middle East Past and Present*. Englewood Cliffs, NJ: Prentice-Hall, 1970.

_____. "What the U.S. Needs to Know about Iran." *World Review* 22 (May 1979):13–19.

Ashraf, Ahmad. "Historical Obstacles to the Development of a Bourgeoisie in Iran." *Iranian Studies* 2 (Spring-Summer 1969):54–78.

Azad, Shahrzad. "Workers' and Peasants' Councils in Iran." *Monthly Review* 32 (October 1980):14–29.

Bahar, M.A. *A Short History of Political Parties*. Tehran: Chap-i Rangin, 1943.

Bakhash, Shaul. *The Reign of the Ayatollahs: Iran and the Islamic Revolution*. New York: Basic Books, 1984.

Banani, Amin. *The Modernization of Iran, 1921–1941*. Stanford: Stanford University Press, 1961.

Bayat, Mangol. "The Iranian Revolution of 1978–79: Fundamentalist or Modern?" *Middle East Journal* 37 (Winter 1983):30–42.

_____. "Iran's Real Revolutionary Leader." *Christian Science Monitor* (24 May 1979):23.

Bayne, Edward Ashley. *Four Ways of Politics: State and Nation in Italy, Somalia, Israel, Iran*. New York: American Universities Field Staff, 1965.

_____. *Persian Kingship in Transition*. New York: American Universities Field Staff, 1968.

Bazargan, Mehdi. *Enghalab-e Iran dar Du Harakat* (The Revolution in Iran in Two Stages). 3d. ed. Tehran: Naraghi, 1363/1984.

Beer, Samuel H., and Adam B. Ulam, eds. *Patterns of Government: The Major Political Systems of Europe*. New York: Random House, 1958.

Behnam, Jamsheed. "Population." In *The Cambridge History of Iran: The Land of Iran*, vol. 1, ed. W.B. Fisher, pp. 468–85. London: Cambridge University Press, 1968.

Benard, Cheryl, and Zalmay Khalilzad. *"The Government of God"—Iran's Islamic Republic*. New York: Columbia University Press, 1984.

Bill, James A. "Iran and the Crisis of '78." *Foreign Affairs* 57 (Winter 1978–79):323–42.

_____. "Modernization and Reform from Above: The Case of Iran." *Journal of Politics* 32 (February 1970):19–40.

_____. "The Plasticity of Informal Politics: The Case of Iran." *Middle East Journal* 27 (Spring 1973):131–51.

_____. *The Politics of Iran: Groups, Classes and Modernization.* Columbus, OH: Charles E. Merrill, 1972.

_____. "Power and Religion in Revolutionary Iran." *Middle East Journal* 36 (Winter 1982):22–47.

_____. "The Social and Economic Foundations of Power in Contemporary Iran." *Middle East Journal* 17 (Autumn 1963):400–413.

_____, and Carl Leiden. *The Middle East: Politics and Power.* Boston: Allyn and Bacon, 1974.

Binder, Leonard. *Iran: Political Development in a Changing Society.* Berkeley and Los Angeles: University of California Press, 1962.

Bird, Kai. "Making Iran Safe for Theocracy." *Nation* (19 May 1979):559–61.

Blaustein, Albert P., and Gilbert H. Flanz, eds. *Constitutions of the Countries of the World,* vol. 7. Dobbs Ferry, NY: Oceana Publications, July 1980.

Braswell, George W., Jr. *To Ride a Magic Carpet.* Nashville: Broadman Press, 1977.

Brown, Archie, and Jack Gray, eds. *Political Culture and Political Change in Communist States.* New York: Holmes and Meier, 1977.

Browne, Edward G. *The Persian Constitutional Movement.* From the Proceedings of the British Academy, vol. 8. London: Oxford University Press, 1918.

_____. *The Persian Revolution: 1905–1909.* London: Cambridge University Press, 1910.

_____. *A Year amongst the Persians: Impressions as to the Life, Character, and Thought of the People of Persia.* London: Adam and Charles Black, 1893.

"Calendar Changed, Casinos Shut Down," *Kayhan* (Tehran), International Edition (28 August 1978):1.

Chelkowski, Peter J. *Ta'ziyeh: Ritual and Drama in Iran.* New York: New York University Press, 1979.

Claiborne, William. "Many Iranians Express Discontent." *Washington Post* (27 July 1979):A14.

Cottam, Richard W. *Nationalism in Iran.* 2d ed. Pittsburgh: University of Pittsburgh Press, 1979.

_____. "Political Party Development in Iran." *Iranian Studies* 1 (Summer 1968):82–95.

_____. "The United States, Iran and the Cold War." *Iranian Studies* 3 (Winter 1970):2–22.

Davidian, Harutiun. "The Application of Some Basic Psychological Theories in the Iranian Cultural Context." *International Social Science Journal* 25 (1973):532–46.

"Document: Constitution of the Islamic Republic of Iran." Introductory note by Rouhollah K. Ramazani. *Middle East Journal* 34 (Spring 1980):181–204.

Easton, David, and Jack Dennis. *Children in the Political System: Origins of Political Legitimacy.* New York: McGraw-Hill, 1969.

Elwell-Sutton, L.P. *Persian Oil: A Study in Power and Politics.* Westport, CT: Greenwood, Press, 1975.

Embassy of the Islamic Republic of Iran. Speech delivered regarding the *Hajj,* by Ruhollah Khumayni, 29 September 1979, 1–4.

Esfandiary, Fereidoun. *The Day of Sacrifice.* New York: McDowell, Obolensky, 1957.

_____. *Identity Card.* New York: Grove Press, 1966.

Fagen, Richard. *The Transformation of Political Culture in Cuba.* Stanford: Stanford University Press, 1969.

Fallaci, Oriana. "An Oriana Fallaci Interview—The Shah of Iran." *New Republic* 169 (1 December 1973):16–21.

Farah, Caesar E. *Islam: Beliefs and Observances.* Woodbury, NY: Barron's, 1970.

Fatemi, Khosrow. "Leadership by Distrust: The Shah's Modus Operandi." *Middle East Journal* 36 (Winter 1982):48–62.

Fatih, Mustafā. *Panjah Sal-e Naft-e Iran* (Fifty Years of Iranian Oil). Tehran: Payam Press, 1358/1979.

Fischer, Michael M.J. *Iran: From Religious Dispute to Revolution.* Cambridge, MA: Harvard University Press, 1980.

Frye, Richard N. "Iran and the Unity of the Muslim World." In *Islam and the West,* ed. Richard N. Frye, pp. 179–93. The Hague: Mouton, 1956.

Gable, Richard W. "Culture and Administration in Iran." *Middle East Journal* 13 (Autumn 1959):407–21.

Geertz, Clifford. "In Search of North Africa." *New York Review of Books* 16 (22 April 1971):20–24.

Godsell, Geoffrey. " 'Rights' Critics Pressure the Shah." *Christian Science Monitor* (2 March 1978):3.

Goitein, S.D. *Studies in Islamic History and Institutions.* Leiden: E.J. Brill, 1966.

Graham, Robert. *Iran: The Illusion of Power.* New York: St. Martin's Press, 1978.

Great Britain. *Correspondence between His Majesty's Government in the United Kingdom and the Persian Government and Related Documents Concerning the Oil Industry in Persia, February 1951 to September 1951.* London: His Majesty's Stationery Office, December 1951.

——————. *Documents on British Foreign Policy, 1919–1939.* First Series, vols. 4 and 13. London: Her Majesty's Stationery Office, 1963.

——————. Foreign Office. *British and Foreign State Papers.* Vol. C. London: Her Majesty's Stationery Office, 1815–1978.

——————. War Office, General Staff. *Daily Review of the Foreign Press.* Series 5, no. 78. London: His Majesty's Stationery Office, 1915–19.

Haas, William S. *Iran.* New York: AMS Press, 1966.

Hairi, Abdul-Hadi. *Shi'ism and Constitutionalism in Iran: A Study of the Role Played by the Persian Residents of Iraq in Iranian Politics.* Leiden: E.J. Brill, 1977.

Harkness, Richard, and Gladys Harkness. "The Mysterious Doings of CIA." *Saturday Evening Post* 227 (6 November 1954):34, 64–68.

Hillmann, Michael C. "Language and Social Distinctions in Iran." In *Modern Iran: The Dialectics of Continuity and Change,* ed. Michael E. Bonine and Nikki R. Keddie, pp. 327–40. Albany: State University of New York Press, 1981.

Hitti, Phillip K. *Islam: A Way of Life.* Minneapolis: University of Minnesota Press, 1970.

Hooglund, Eric J. *Land and Revolution in Iran, 1960–1980.* Austin, University of Texas Press, 1982.

Hottinger, Arnold. "Iran in the Melting Pot." *Swiss Review of World Affairs* 28 (September 1978):6–8.

Huntington, Samuel P. *Political Order in Changing Societies.* New Haven: Yale University Press, 1968.

"Iran: Dervish in Pin-Striped Suit." *Time* (4 June 1951):29–35.

"Iran: Expropriation." *Time* (7 May 1951):35.

"Iran: The New Crisis of American Hegemony." *Monthly Review* 30 (February 1979):1–24.

Issawi, Charles, ed. *The Economic History of Iran, 1800–1914.* Chicago: University of Chicago Press, 1971.

Jackson, A.V. Williams. *Zoroastrian Studies: The Iranian Religion and Various Monographs.* New York: Columbia University Press, 1928.

Jacobs, Norman. *The Sociology of Development: Iran as an Asian Case Study.* New York: Praeger, 1966.

Kamshad, H. *Modern Persian Prose Literature*. London: Cambridge University Press, 1966.

Karpat, Kemal H., ed. *Political and Social Thought in the Contemporary Middle East*. New York: Praeger, 1968.

Kasravi, Ahmad. *Tarikh-i Mashruteh-i Iran* (A History of the Iranian Constitution). Tehran: Amir Kabir Press, 1340/1961.

Katouzian, Homayoun. "Nationalist Trends in Iran, 1921–1926." *International Journal of Middle East Studies* 10 (November 1979):533–51.

Kayhan (Tehran), International Edition (5 June 1963).

Kayhan (Tehran), Persian Edition (17 March 1976).

Kayhan (Tehran), International Edition (26 October 1976).

Keddie, Nikki R. "Iran: Is 'Modernization' the Message?" *Middle East Review* 11 (Spring 1979):55–56.

——————. "The Iranian Power Structure and Social Change, 1800–1969: An Overview." *International Journal of Middle East Studies* 2 (January 1971):3–20.

——————. *Religion and Rebellion in Iran: The Tobacco Protest of 1891–1892*. London: Frank Cass, 1966.

——————. *Roots of Revolution: An Interpretive History of Modern Iran*. New Haven: Yale University Press, 1981.

——————. "The Roots of the Ulama's Power in Modern Iran." In *Scholars, Saints and Sufis*, ed. Nikki R. Keddie, pp. 211–29. Berkeley: University of California Press, 1972.

Khumayni, Ruhollah. *Hokumat-e Eslami* (Islamic Government). Najaf: n.p., 1350/1971.

——————. *Islam and Revolution: Writings and Declarations of Imam Khomeini*. Translated and annotated by Hamid Algar. Berkeley: Mizan Press, 1981.

——————. *Kashf al-Asrar* (Unveiling of Secrets). N.p.: 1323/1944.

Kluckhohn, Clyde. "Myths and Rituals: A General Theory." In *Reader in Comparative Religion: An Anthropological Approach,* ed. William A. Lessa and Evon Z. Vogt, pp. 135–51. Evanston, IL: Row, Peterson, 1958.

——————, and Henry A. Murray. "Personality Formation: The Determinants." In *Personality in Nature, Society, and Culture,* 2d ed., ed. Clyde Kluckhohn and Henry A. Murray, pp. 53–67. New York: Alfred A. Knopf, 1956.

Koury, Enver M., and Charles G. MacDonald, eds. *Revolution in Iran: A Reappraisal.* Hyattsville, MD: Institute of Middle Eastern and North African Affairs, 1982.

Kroeber, Alfred, and Clyde Kluckhohn. *Culture: A Critical Review of Concepts and Definitions.* New York: Random House, 1952.

Lambton, Ann K.S. *Islamic Society in Persia.* London: Oxford University Press, 1954.

——————. *The Persian Land Reform, 1962–1966.* Oxford: Clarendon Press, 1969.

——————. "A Reconsideration of the Position of the Marja' al-Taqlid and the Religious Institution." *Studia Islamica* 20 (1964):115–35.

Lehman, Edward W. "On the Concept of Political Culture: A Theoretical Reassessment." *Social Forces* 50 (March 1972):361–70.

Leites, Nathan. *A Study of Bolshevism.* Glencoe, IL: Free Press, 1953.

Lenczowski, George, ed. *Iran under the Pahlavis.* Stanford: Hoover Institution Press, 1978.

——————. *The Middle East in World Affairs.* 4th ed. Ithaca: Cornell University Press, 1980.

Lengyel, Emil. *The Changing Middle East.* New York: John Day, 1960.

Looney, Robert E. *Iran at the End of the Century: A Hegelian Forecast.* Lexington, MA: D.C. Heath, 1977.

Machiavelli, Niccolò. *The Prince.* Trans. Luigi Ricci. New York: Modern Library, 1940.

Majmoo-ah-yeh Ah'd Nāmah-haye Tarīkhee-a Iran: Az Ah'd Hakhamanashee tah Asr Pahlavi, 559 B.C.–1320 (Compendium of Iran's Historical Treaties: From the Time of Achaemenid to the Dawn of Pahlavi, 559 B.C.–1942). Tehran: Imperial Foreign Ministry Publications.

"Man of the Year: Challenge of the East." *Time* (7 January 1952):18–21.

Mansfield, Peter, ed. *The Middle East: A Political and Economic Survey.* 5th ed. London: Oxford University Press, 1980.

McClelland, David C. "National Character and Economic Growth in Turkey and Iran." In *Communications and Political Development,* ed. Lucian W. Pye, pp. 152–81. Princeton, NJ: Princeton University Press, 1963.

Miller, William Green. "Political Organization in Iran: From *Dowreh* to Political Party," Part I and Part II. *Middle East Journal* 23 (Spring and Summer 1969):159–67, 343–50.

Millspaugh, Arthur C. *Americans in Persia.* Washington, D.C.: Brookings Institution, 1946.

Minorsky, Vladimir. "Iran: Opposition, Martyrdom, and Revolt." In *Unity and Variety in Muslim Civilization,* ed. Gustave E. von Grunebaum, pp. 183–206. Chicago: University of Chicago Press, 1955.

Morier, James. *The Adventures of Hajji Baba of Ispahan.* Ed. C. J. Wills. London: Lawrence and Bullen, 1897.

al-Mulk, Nizam. *Siyasat-nama or Siyar al-Muluk* (The Book of Government or Rules for Kings). Trans. Hubert Drake. London: Routledge and Kegan Paul, 1960.

Nasr, Seyyed Hossein. *Ideals and Realities of Islam.* New York: Praeger, 1967.

_____. "Ithna Ashari Shi'ism and Iranian Islam." In *Religion in the Middle East: Three Religions in Concord and Conflict,* ed. A.J. Arberry, pp. 96–118. London: Cambridge University Press, 1969.

Pahlavi, Mohammad Reza. *Answer to History.* New York: Stein and Day, 1980.

_____. *Mission for My Country.* London: Hutchinson, 1961.

Pahlavi Library Publications. *Bargozide-i az Neveshte-ha va Sokhanan-e Shah-an-Shah Aryamehr* (A Selection of Writings and Speeches by the Shah of Shahs, Light of the Aryans). Tehran: Pahlavi Library Publications, 1347/1968.

Parsons, Talcott. *Structure and Process in Modern Societies.* New York: Free Press, 1960.

Patai, Raphael. *Golden River to Golden Road: Society, Culture, and Change in the Middle East.* 3d ed. Philadelphia: University of Pennsylvania Press, 1969.

Peaslee, Amos J. *Constitutions of Nations.* 2d ed. Vol. 2. The Hague: Martinus Nijhoff, 1956.

Pfaff, Richard H. "Disengagement from Traditionalism in Turkey and Iran." In *The Contemporary Middle East: Tradition and Innovation,* ed. Benjamin Rivlin and Joseph S. Szyliowicz, pp. 417–28. New York: Random House, 1965.

Pranger, Robert J. "Political and Economic Balance in Iran." *Current History* 38 (May 1960):278–84.

Pye, Lucian W. "Culture and Political Science: Problems in the Evaluation of the Concept of Political Culture." *Social Science Quarterly* 53 (September 1972):285–96.

_____. "Introduction: Political Culture and Political Development." In *Political Culture and Political Development,* ed. Lucian W. Pye and Sidney Verba, pp. 3–26. Princeton: Princeton University Press, 1965.

_____. *Politics, Personality, and Nation Building: Burma's Search for Identity.* New Haven: Yale University Press, 1962.

_____, and Sidney Verba, eds. *Political Culture and Political Development.* Princeton: Princeton University Press, 1965.

Rahman, Fazlur. *Islam.* 2d ed. Chicago: University of Chicago Press, 1979.

Ramazani, Rouhollah K. *The Foreign Policy of Iran, 1500-1941.* Charlottesville: University Press of Virginia, 1966.

Roosevelt, Kermit. *Countercoup: The Struggle for the Control of Iran.* New York: McGraw-Hill, 1979.

Rouleau, Eric. "Khomeini's Iran." *Foreign Affairs* 59 (Fall 1980):1-20.

Rubin, Barry. *Paved with Good Intentions: The American Experience and Iran.* London: Oxford University Press, 1980.

Rudolph-Touba, Jacquiline. *Marriage and the Family in Iran.* Tehran: Institute for Social Studies and Research, University of Tehran, 1972.

Sadiq, Issa Khan. *Modern Persia and Her Educational System.* Studies of the International Institute of Teachers College, Columbia University, no. 14. New York: Bureau of Publications, Columbia University, 1931.

Sahib al-Zamani, Nasir al-Din. *Javani-yi Purranj* (Suffering Youth). With short versions in English and German. Tehran: Ataii Press, 1346/1967.

Saikal, Amin. *The Rise and Fall of the Shah.* Princeton: Princeton University Press, 1980.

Savory, Roger M. "Iran: A 2,500-Year Historical and Cultural Tradition." In *Iranian Civilization and Culture,* ed. Charles J. Adams, pp. 77-89. Montreal: McGill University Institute of Islamic Studies, 1972.

Schmitt, David E. *The Irony of Irish Democracy.* Lexington, MA: D.C. Heath, 1973.

Shafaq, S.R. "Patriotic Poetry in Modern Iran." *Middle East Journal* 6 (Autumn 1952):417-28.

"The Shah's Divided Land." *Time* (18 September 1978):35-36.

Shari'ati, Ali. *Hajj.* Trans. Somayyah and Yaser. Bedford, OH: Free Islamic Literatures, 1977.

_____. *On the Sociology of Islam.* Trans. Hamid Algar. Berkeley: Mizan Press, 1979.

_____. *Tamaddon va Tajaddod* (Civilization and Modernization). N.p., 1352/1973.

_____. *Ummat va Imamat* (People and Leadership). Tehran: n.p., 1350/1971.

Shari'at, Dr. B. "State or Free Enterprise." *Tehran Economist,* 5 March 1965.

Shibutani, Tamotsu, and Kian M. Kwan. *Ethnic Stratification.* New York: Macmillan, 1965.

Sick, Gary. *All Fall Down: America's Tragic Encounter with Iran.* New York: Random House, 1985.

Siddique, Kaukab. "Islamic Iran: A Society in Transition." *Islamic Revolution* 1 (October 1979):4-17.

Spiro, Melford. "Social Systems, Personality, and Functional Analysis." In *Studying Personality Cross-Culturally,* ed. Bert Kaplan, pp. 93-127. Evanston, IL: Row, Peterson, 1961.

Sutherland, E. "Pastoralism, Nomadism and the Social Anthropology of Iran." In *The Cambridge History of Iran: The Land of Iran,* vol. 1, ed. W.B. Fisher, pp. 611-83. London: Cambridge University Press, 1968.

Tabataba'i, Allamah Sayyid Muhammad Husayn. *Shi'ite Islam.* Trans. and ed. with an introduction and notes by Seyyed Hossein Nasr. Albany: State University of New York Press, 1975.

Ta'limat-i Dini Bara-yi Sal-i Panjum-i Dabistan va Sal-i Shishum-i Dabistan (The Book of Religious Instruction for the Fifth Year of Primary School and the Sixth Year of Primary School). Tehran: n.p., 1346/1967-68.

Thaiss, Gustav. "Religious Symbolism and Social Change: The Drama of Husain." In *Scholars, Saints and Sufis,* ed. Nikki R. Keddie, pp. 349-66. Berkeley: University of California Press, 1972.

_____. "Unity and Discord: The Symbol of Husayn in Iran." In *Iranian Civilization and Culture,* ed. Charles J. Adams, pp. 111–19. Montreal: McGill University Institute of Islamic Studies, 1972.

Tucker, Robert C. "Culture, Political Culture, and Communist Society." *Political Science Quarterly,* 88 (June 1973):173–90.

Ullman, Richard H. *Anglo-Soviet Relations, 1917–1921.* Vol. 3. Princeton: Princeton University Press, 1972.

U.S. Department of Commerce. *Translations on Near East and North Africa: Khomeyni Interview on Islamic Revolutionary Movement.* No. 1909. Arlington, VA: Joint Publications Research Service, no. 72813, 13 February 1979.

U.S. Department of Health, Education and Welfare. *Education in Iran: Studies in Comparative Education,* by Abdul H.K. Sassani. OE-14081, Bulletin 1963, no. 18. Washington, D.C.: Government Printing Office, 1963.

Upton, Joseph M. *The History of Modern Iran: An Interpretation.* Cambridge, MA: Harvard University Press, 1961.

Van Nieuwenhuijze, C.A.O. *Sociology of the Middle East: A Stocktaking and Interpretation.* Leiden: E.J. Brill, 1971.

Verba, Sidney. "Conclusion: Comparative Political Culture." In *Political Culture and Political Development,* ed. Lucian W. Pye and Sidney Verba, pp. 512–60. Princeton, NJ: Princeton University Press, 1965.

Watt, W. Montgomery. *Islamic Political Thought: The Basic Concepts.* Edinburgh: Edinburgh University Press, 1968.

Weber, Max. *The Protestant Ethic and the Spirit of Capitalism.* Trans. Talcott Parsons. New York: Charles Scribner's Sons, 1958.

Westwood, Andrew F. "Politics of Distrust in Iran." *Annals of the American Academy of Political and Social Science* 358 (March 1965):123–35.

White, Leslie A. *The Science of Culture.* New York: Farrar, Straus and Cudahy, 1949.

Wiatr, Jerzy J. "The Civic Culture from a Marxist-Sociological Perspective." In *The Civic Culture Revisited,* ed. Gabriel A. Almond and Sidney Verba, pp. 103–23. Boston: Little, Brown, 1980.

Wilber, Donald N. *Contemporary Iran.* London: Thames and Hudson, 1963.

_____. *Iran, Past and Present: From Monarchy to Islamic Republic.* 9th ed. Princeton: Princeton University Press, 1981.

Young, T. Cuyler. "The Social Support of Current Iranian Policy." *Middle East Journal* 6 (Spring 1952):125–43.

Zabih, Sepehr. *The Communist Movement in Iran.* Berkeley: University of California Press, 1966.

_____. *Iran since the Revolution.* Baltimore: John Hopkins Press, 1982.

Zaehner, R.C. *The Dawn and Twilight of Zoroastrianism.* New York: G.P. Putnam's Sons, 1961.

Zarrīnkūb, Abd al-Hossein. *Bamdād-e Eslam* (The Dawn of Islam). 2d ed. Tehran: Amir Kabir, 1353/1974.

Zonis, Marvin. "Higher Education and Social Change: Problems and Prospects." In *Iran Faces the Seventies,* ed. Ehsan Yar-Shater, pp. 217–58. New York: Praeger, 1971.

_____. *The Political Elite of Iran.* Princeton: Princeton University Press, 1971.

Index